Hoover Institution Studies

The Jerusalem Question, 1917-1968

The Jerusalem Question, 1917-1968

H. Eugene Bovis

Hoover Institution Press
Stanford University
Stanford, California

Hoover Institution Studies 29 (Policy 1)
© 1971 by the Board of Trustees of the Leland Stanford Junior University
All rights reserved
Library of Congress Catalog Card Number: 73-149796
Standard Book Number 8179-3291-7
Printed in the United States of America

Policy Studies

Policy Studies comprise a new series of Hoover Institution Press books designed to focus on areas of tension in the world today, to apprise the reader of the factors which underlie these tensions, and to evaluate alternative courses of action available to policy-makers. Occasionally, as with the present volume, problems are studied from the perspective of an international organization. Works in the new series average 150 pages in length.

Opinions or recommendations are those of the author and do not necessarily represent those of the Hoover Institution.

Policy Studies will be incorporated into the Hoover Institution Studies Series and will be mailed automatically to customers with standing orders for the Studies Series. Standing orders may be placed for the Policy Study Series alone.

CONTENTS

Acknowledgements

This study was originally prepared as a doctoral dissertation, and it would be inappropriate if acknowledgements were not made of the encouragement and assistance given by the chairman and the members of the supervising committee: Dr. Harry N. Howard, Dr. Kerim K. Key, and Dr. Mary E. Bradshaw. I also wish to express my appreciation to Miss Georgiana Stevens, Dr. George Rentz, Dr. Shepard Jones, Dr. Harold W. Glidden, Dr. James H. Bahti, Mr. Richard B. Parker, Mr. Henry Precht, Mrs. Gloria Dulberg, and former Assistant Secretary of State Raymond A. Hare, who kindly read the draft and offered many helpful suggestions. It should be made clear, however, that the views presented in this study are my own and not necessarily those of the individuals mentioned here nor of the Department of State or the United States Government. In addition, an immense vote of thanks is due my wife, Beatrice, who not only offered many helpful comments but assumed the particularly laborious task of typing both the draft and the final text.

Acknowledgement is made of the permission granted by Beaverbrook Newspapers Ltd. to quote from *The Truth About The Peace Treaties* by David Lloyd George, to the Catholic Association for International Peace to quote from *The Internationalization of Jerusalem*, and to Her Majesty's Stationery Office to quote from Command Papers 964, 1708, 1785, 5479, and 5854.

Introduction

Jerusalem holds a place of honor in the hearts of the followers of the three major monotheistic religions—Judaism, Christianity, and Islam. Here is situated the Wailing Wall, a remnant of the western wall of the parvis surrounding the First and Second Temples.* On the spot where the Temples stood there are now the Muslim sanctuaries of the Haram al-Sharif. One of these, the Dome of the Rock, stands over the spot from which tradition says Muhammad made his night journey into Heaven, and consequently Jerusalem is considered by muslims to be the third most sacred city in the world, after Mecca and Medina. Indeed, Muhammad originally taught his followers to pray facing Jerusalem and only later did the Ka'bah in Mecca replace it. Here in Jerusalem is also situated the Church of the Holy Sepulchre, which stands over the supposed sites where Jesus was crucified and buried. Because of these shrines, which are only the most important of many in Jerusalem, men and governments have long taken a special interest in the city's fate.

The Jerusalem question has two basic elements: Who is to exercise sovereignty over the city itself, and how are the Holy Places to be administered? The two elements are of course related, but they have not always been of equal importance at the same time. For almost 700 years prior to World War I, it was primarily the question of the Holy Places that figured in the diplomacy of the European powers, since Jerusalem was situated after 1517 within the Ottoman Empire and before 1517 within the confines of other Muslim empires. World War I, however, ended the Ottoman Empire and placed Jerusalem once more in Christian hands, and the question of sovereignty became active again, along with the question of the administration of the Holy Places. Even so, governments often attach more importance to one aspect than the other, as this study

*In Hebrew, the Wailing Wall is called Hakotel Hamaaravi (Western Wall) and some writers refer to it in English as the Western Wall. For the sake of convenience, the more familiar term Wailing Wall will be used in this study.

will show. In some cases, governments have used the Jerusalem question to support or advance other interests of a more secular nature.

From World War I until 1936, Jerusalem was primarily a European question, with Great Britain, France, Italy, and the Vatican, in one combination or another, as the main contenders. By 1936, Palestine had become the object of a struggle between two nationalisms, Zionism and Palestinian Arab nationalism, and Jerusalem had come to be considered by the two main contenders as a prize for the victor. In solutions proposed after 1936, the mandatory and other European powers sought to remove Jerusalem from this context and to give it a separate regime. This, in fact, was the intent of the Palestine partition plan adopted by the United Nations on November 29, 1947. However, the U.N. seriously misjudged the intensity of the Arab-Zionist struggle when it assumed that a solution could be imposed from the outside against the wishes of one or both of the contenders without the use of force.

By the end of 1948, Jerusalem had become primarily an Arab-Israel question. To be sure, other interests were still involved, but the main contenders were no longer European, or even Christian for that matter. Jerusalem was then divided between Jordan and Israel and the prevailing situation was not considered unsatisfactory at the time by either. However, the inability of the Christian powers, particularly the Catholic powers, to recognize the changed nature of the Jerusalem question and their own diminished role in it prevented the U.N. from giving the arrangement the blessing of the international community. After a life of nineteen years, this arrangement has crumbled and a new one is needed. Whatever the new arrangement turns out to be, it will clearly have to be made within the Arab-Israel context, or perhaps, like the previous one, only within the Israel-Jordan context. Other interests will eventually have to be harmonized with whatever that solution turns out to be.

Although the Jerusalem question has become deeply enmeshed today in the Arab-Israel question, it is not necessarily congruent with it. It is an international problem with a history of its own, often running parallel with the other question but just as often completely transcending it. The purpose of this study is to tell that story as it has evolved since World War I. Because the focus here is on Jerusalem, no attempt will be made to narrate the history of the Arab-Israel struggle except insofar as it is necessary to give continuity to the story of the Jerusalem question.

As with any diplomatic problem, it would be foolish to suppose that there is only one possible solution. Similarly, there is seldom an ideal solution to any problem. However, the essential elements of a reasonable settlement should be visible after fifty years of the Jerusalem question. An attempt will therefore be made to indicate what these essential elements are and to see how the various solutions often put forth measure up in terms of the essentials.

This study was prepared in 1968, and the narrative ceases with the spring of that year. Nothing has happened over the past two years, however, to change the lines of the study. Mention should perhaps be made of one event during this period which points up what has just been said about the importance of Jerusalem. On August 21, 1969, a young Christian sheep hand from Australia, Michael Rohan, set fire to the al-Aqsa Mosque, which is one of the Muslim sanctuaries of the Haram al-Sharif. Rohan told the Israeli authorities after his arrest that he had been instructed by God to burn the Mosque so that the Temple of Solomon could be rebuilt on the site. The reactions to this event were predictable. The Israelis were embarrassed that such a thing could have happened while Jerusalem was under their control. Rohan was placed on trial, found to be mentally unbalanced, and has been confined to a mental institution. The Islamic World was disturbed about the safety of its shrines in Jerusalem. The Arabs treated the event as proof that the Israelis were out to destroy the Mosque and rebuild the Temple. Arab bitterness was deepened and the drama of the Jerusalem question was heightened.

Chapter 1

The Return to Christian Hands

Interests of the Big Powers

On December 9, 1917, British troops occupied Jerusalem, and the Holy City passed into Christian hands for the first time since the rule of Frederick II as King of Jerusalem was extinguished in 1244. The question of the future of Jerusalem now lay with the Western powers and was to all intents and purposes bound up with the question of harmonizing their interests in Palestine as a whole.

On the eve of World War I, Britain, France, and Russia had long-standing interests of one sort or another in Palestine and each was therefore reluctant to see Palestine come under the exclusive control of either of the other two. France had acquired in the course of time after 1535 the position of protector of Latin Christians in the Ottoman Empire, while Russia had asserted the right to protect Orthodox Christians. Protection, however, had often meant protection of the Latins against the Orthodox or the Orthodox against the Latins, rather than protection against the Ottoman authorities.

This was particularly so in the case of the Holy Places in Jerusalem and Bethlehem. Prior to the Crusades, the Orthodox Patriarchate had been the chief custodian of the Church of the Holy Sepulchre in Jerusalem and the Church of the Nativity in Bethlehem. During the Crusades, however, the Latins gained control, which they apparently maintained until the Ottoman conquest of Palestine in 1517. From this time on, the Ottoman authorities played the Latins and the Orthodox off against each other, the result being that first one and then the other held the primacy in accordance with which could produce the most revenue for the Ottoman coffers or bring the most foreign pressure to bear. The capitulations to France in 1604 and 1740 confirmed the Latins in possession of the Holy Sepulchre and Calvary, the Church of the Nativity,

and the Church of the Virgin. On the other hand, the Orthodox Patriarch of Jerusalem, Theophanes III, obtained a *firman* in 1637 in favor of the Orthodox. Again, in 1757, while
the Europeans were busily engaged in the Seven Years' War,
the Orthodox seized control of those Holy Places they
claimed in Jerusalem and Bethlehem and secured a *firman*
from the Sultan recognizing the new state of affairs.

Here the matter had stood until 1847, when a silver star,
bearing a Latin inscription attesting to Latin rights to the
supposed birthplace of Christ, disappeared from the Church
of the Nativity in Bethlehem. This provided the French with
an opportunity to reopen the question of Latin rights. A Franco-Ottoman Commission was appointed to examine the
question of rights of the various Christian bodies. Russia,
however, objected on behalf of the Orthodox and insisted on
the maintenance of the status quo. The Franco-Ottoman
Commission was then replaced with a purely Ottoman Commission. In accordance with the Commission's recommendations, the Sultan issued a *firman* in 1852 confirming
the status quo but making a few minor concessions to the
Latins.

By 1914, however, France had interests other than purely
religious ones in the Holy Land. The Entente Cordiale of 1904
had marked the end of French ambition in Egypt, and France
had shifted the focus of its Near Eastern policy to Syria,
roughly defined in French thinking of the time as extending
from Alexandretta to al-Arish. French interest in Latin and
Uniat Christians had won a large measure of influence in the
Lebanon. French educational efforts added to this influence
and prestige throughout *la Syrie intégrale*. In addition,
French investment in the area greatly exceeded that of any
other country, and on the eve of World War I plans were
being formulated for an ambitious public works program, including harbor works in Haifa and Jaffa and a southward ex-
tension of the Syrian railway to connect with the French-
owned railway between Jaffa and Jerusalem. If French naval
bases were established in Alexandretta and Haifa, French
naval power in the Mediterranean would be notably enhanced. Expansion of the rail lines would greatly facilitate the
movement of troops, and France would become a power to be
reckoned with in the Eastern Mediterranean.

While Great Britain was generally regarded as protector of the Protestants, Jews, and Druzes in the Ottoman Empire, British interests in Palestine during this period were also primarily strategic. Great Britain was most desirous of preventing a rival imperial power from occupying the eastern approaches to the Suez Canal. Prior to World War I, British concern on this score was largely satisfied by the sovereignty of Europe's "sick man" over Palestine and by the buffer zone provided by the practically empty expanse of the Sinai Peninsula, which had been brought under Egyptian administration in 1892 at the instigation of Lord Cromer. However, if a European power, with the resources and ambitions of France, were installed in Palestine, British concern for Egypt's and the Canal's defense would no longer be allayed. Despite the Entente Cordiale and the Anglo-French alliance during World War I, it was not certain that Great Britain could count on France's benevolence forever. German influence in the Ottoman Empire during World War I and the Turkish attempt to cross the Canal in February of 1915 only served to underscore the danger inherent in having an unfriendly power in Palestine.

Soon after the outbreak of World War I, Great Britain, France, and Russia began consultations as to the disposition to be made of the various portions of the Ottoman Empire at the close of the war. In view of the long-standing interests of the three powers in the Holy Land and the Holy Places, the secret agreements which they concluded provided that the ports of Haifa and Acre were to be given to Great Britain, that an international administration was to be established in Palestine west of the Jordan between Haifa and Gaza, and that Great Britain was to have paramount influence in the rest of the area bordering on the Sinai Peninsula. According to the Tripartite (Sykes-Picot) Agreement of mid-1916, the form of the international administration was to be decided upon after consultation among the three powers and subsequently in consultation with the Allies and the representatives of the Sharif of Mecca. The agreement of St. Jean de Maurienne in 1917 associated Italy with the three powers that would consult initially on the form of international administration to be installed in Palestine.[1]

In the meantime, Great Britain was engaged in two other

sets of negotiations, one with Sharif Husayn of Mecca and one with the Zionists. An exchange of correspondence took place between Sir Henry McMahon, British High Commissioner in Cairo, and the Sharif from July 1915 to March 1916. The purpose was to induce the Arabs to revolt against the Turks in exchange for a British pledge to support Arab independence after the war. In addition, it was reasoned that the erection of an Arab state centered on the Holy Places of Islam and under British influence would not only serve as added protection for the British route to India but would, with the disappearance of the Ottoman Empire, help assure peace and tranquility among Great Britain's other Muslim subjects, notably in India and Egypt. Sir Henry, on instructions from his government, promised British recognition and support for the "independence of the Arabs" in the Ottoman territories south of the 37th parallel. It was understood that the Arabs would seek the advice and guidance of Great Britain only and that "when the situation admits, Great Britain will give to the Arabs her advice and will assist them to establish what may appear to be the most suitable forms of government in those territories." Husayn demanded the Mediterranean and the Red Sea as the western boundary. McMahon agreed to the Red Sea boundary but excluded the coastal belt of Syria "lying to the west of the districts of Damascus, Homs, Hama, and Aleppo."[2] While there is little doubt that this meant the exclusion of Lebanon and the area northward, it left considerable uncertainty whether Palestine was also excluded, and this point remains the subject of much controversy. The provision in the Sykes-Picot Agreement, concluded subsequently, for consultation with the Sharif on the form of international regime to be installed in Palestine does not shed any light on this point. In any event, the British Government put forth its own interpretation of the McMahon pledge, and Colonial Secretary Winston Churchill declared in London in 1922: "This reservation has always been regarded by His Majesty's Government as covering the vilayet of Beirut and the independent sanjak of Jerusalem. The whole of Palestine west of the Jordan was thus excluded from Sir H. McMahon's pledge."[3]

The second set of negotiations, with the Zionists, culminated in the Balfour Declaration of November 2, 1917. Lloyd

4

George had apparently toyed with the idea of a Jewish commonwealth in Palestine under the British Crown in January 1915. Sporadic contacts between British officials and Zionist leaders took place throughout the early years of the war, but it was not until 1917 that the question was considered in earnest. Russia was shaken by revolution in March 1917 and Great Britain was apprehensive lest the Provisional Government decide to make a separate peace. Since a number of the new Russian leaders were Jews, it was suggested that a declaration in favor of a Jewish national home in Palestine might bolster the Provisional Government's determination to stay in the war. It was also suggested that such a declaration would assure the loyalty of the Jews in the Allied countries and attract the sympathy of the large number of Jews in the Central powers. In addition, some British statesmen came to believe that, if given a chance, many Jews would flock to Palestine after the war to settle and that if Great Britain supported the idea of a Jewish national home in Palestine, it might be able to establish a British protectorate over the country, thus assuring exclusive British control rather than international control. The Balfour Declaration would thus give moral weight to a British claim to be the protecting power, just as the military conquest then in progress would give the British claim a material basis.

At the close of the war, the Arab areas of the Ottoman Empire were in British hands and the Bolshevik government in Russia had repudiated the secret treaties concluded during the war and had thus removed itself from the running in the Near East. The French came to suspect that the British had designs on the whole area. It was against this background that French Premier Georges Clemenceau and British Prime Minister Lloyd George agreed at a meeting in London in December 1918 that Mosul would be transferred to British control and that British control could be substituted in Palestine for the international control provided for by the Sykes-Picot Agreement. The meeting took place without a secretary and the agreement was not reduced to writing. It is therefore not clear what undertakings or understanding Lloyd George gave to Clemenceau other than support for French claims in the areas (except Mosul) assigned to it under the Sykes-Picot Agreement. The French later claimed that Clemenceau's agreement to British control in Palestine was given on condition that the question of the Holy Places be resolved to the satisfaction of France.[4] In any event, as a result of the Clemenceau-Lloyd George agreement, the Allied Supreme Council decided on April 25, 1920, that the Palestine mandate would be assigned to the United Kingdom.

The Holy Places Question After the War

Other eyes were also watching the Palestine question. At the close of the war, the Vatican was diplomatically isolated in Europe. Relations with Italy had been strained since the Italian seizure of Rome in 1879; relations with France had been broken in 1904 and the Vatican had been alienated even further in 1905 with the separation of church and state in France; and the war had seen the collapse of the German Empire and the Austro-Hungarian Empire. The Vatican now sought a rapprochement with France as a means of escaping its isolation.[5] Further, the Vatican believed that a renewed French-Vatican alliance would further the interests of both in the Near East, particularly in Palestine. The Holy Land was in the hands of the Allies and the voice of the Orthodox was muted by Russia's temporary withdrawal from world politics. The time was now ripe not only to revise the status quo of 1852 but to assert the power of Christian presence in Palestine and bring the "dissidents" into communion with Rome.[6]

By the end of 1918, however, the Vatican was apprehensive lest the national home provisions of the Balfour Declaration diminish even further the influence of Christians in the Holy Land and perhaps even compromise the already existing rights of Latins in the Holy Places. Representations were made to the British Government early in March 1919 in favor of allowing immigrants from Malta to settle in Palestine in order to strengthen the Latin position.[7] In an allocution to the College of Cardinals on March 10, 1919, Pope Benedict XV declared:

> But there is one matter on which We are specially anxious and that is the fate of the Holy Places, on account of the special dignity and importance for which they are so venerated by every Christian. Who can ever tell the full story of all the

efforts of Our Predecessors to free them from the dominion of infidels, the heroic deeds and the blood shed by the Christians of the West through the centuries? And now that, amid the rejoicing of all good men, they have finally returned into the hands of the Christians, Our anxiety is most keen as to the decisions which the Peace Congress at Paris is soon to take concerning them. For surely it would be a terrible grief for Us and for all the Christian faithful if infidels were placed in a privileged and prominent position; much more if those most holy sanctuaries of the Christian religion were given to the charge of non-Christians.[8]

The question of the Holy Places came up when the peace treaty with Turkey was discussed by the Allied Supreme Council in London in February 1920 and at San Remo in April 1920.[9] Alexandre Millerand had succeeded Clemenceau as Premier of France in January 1920 and Paul Cambon had become his Foreign Minister. They maintained that Clemenceau's agreement in December 1918 to the substitution of British control for international control in Palestine had been given on condition that the question of the Holy Places be settled to the satisfaction of France, and they therefore demanded a special position for France in reference to the protection of the Holy Places. Cambon said at the London conference that the Holy Places had been in the hands of the French since the fifteenth century and that even the Vatican had acknowledged the right of France to a protectorate over the Holy Places.

Both Lloyd George and Francesco Nitti, who had succeeded Vittorio Orlando as Italian Premier in June 1919, objected to the French demand. Lloyd George asserted that the French proposal would amount to two mandatories in Palestine and such an arrangement would make it impossible for Great Britain to administer the country. Nitti said that Italy had never recognized the French protectorate over the Holy Places, and that in any event existing rights had been created by necessities stemming from a Muslim occupation. He thought that with Great Britain's assumption of the mandate no protection of the Holy Places would be required, and that no country should have any special privilege in regard to them or in regard to religious communities. As for individuals, he thought each should turn to his own government for whatever protection he needed. On the other hand, Nitti was of the opinion that the various religious claims in the Holy Places should be studied. At the San Remo conference, he suggested the following addition to the Turkish treaty:

> All privileges and all prerogatives in regard to religious communities will terminate. The Mandatory Power undertakes to appoint, in as short a time as possible, a special commission to study and determine all questions and claims, concerning the different religious communities. Account will be taken, in the composition of this commission of the religious interests involved. The Chairman of the Commission will be appointed by the Council of the League of Nations.[10]

Lloyd George accepted the Italian proposal. In the end, the French accepted it and agreed not to assert any special privileges in Palestine, provided the first sentence of the Italian proposal was dropped. Millerand explained that in view of the keen sensitivity of the French nation, it would be better if the French delegation did not have to state formally that it had agreed to surrender long-existing rights and privileges. The Italian proposal became the second paragraph of Article 95 of the Treaty of Sèvres, which was signed by Turkey on August 10, 1920.[11]

The U.K. attempted to embody these decisions in the mandate instrument. In the draft presented for the approval of the League of Nations, Article 8 specified: "The immunities and privileges of foreigners, including the benefits of consular jurisdiction and protection as formerly enjoyed by capitulation or usage in the Ottoman Empire, are definitely abrogated in Palestine." Article 14 read:

> In accordance with Article 95 of the Treaty of Peace with Turkey, the Mandatory undertakes to appoint as soon as possible a special Commission to study and regulate all questions and claims relating to the different religious communities. In the composition of this Commission the religious interests concerned will be taken into account. The chairman of the Commission will be appointed by the Council of the League of Nations. It will be the duty of this Commission to ensure that certain Holy Places, religious buildings or sites, regarded with special veneration by the adherents of one particular religion,

are entrusted to the permanent control of suitable bodies representing the adherents of the religion concerned.

The selection of the Holy Places, religious buildings or sites so to be entrusted shall be made by the Commission, subject to the approval of the Mandatory.

In all cases dealt with under this Article, however, the right and duty of the Mandatory to maintain order and decorum in the place concerned shall not be affected, and the buildings and sites will be subject to the provisions of such laws relating to public monuments as may be enacted in Palestine with the approval of the Mandatory.

The rights of control conferred under this Article will be guaranteed by the League of Nations.[12]

In addition, Article 28 provided that in the event of the termination of the mandate, the Council of the League of Nations should make necessary arrangements for the guarantee by the League of rights in the Holy Places.

Adoption of the Mandate

Although the draft mandate for Palestine was presented to the Council of the League of Nations in December 1920, it was not considered by the League Council until July 1922, owing to other complications, namely U.S. objections to a British mandate over Palestine without sufficient guarantees of American rights and French objections to approval of the Palestine mandate until the mandate over Syria was approved. Approval of the Syrian mandate was being held up by Italian-French negotiations over Italian rights in Syria. British-American negotiations dragged on until early May 1922 before agreement was reached. The U.S. insisted, in particular, that Article 8 be revised to allow for the revival of capitulations in the event that the mandate was terminated. After a prolonged exchange of correspondence,[13] Article 8 was revised to read:

The immunities and privileges of foreigners, including the benefits of consular jurisdiction and protection as formerly enjoyed by Capitulation or usage in the Ottoman Empire, are suspended in Palestine, but shall be revived immediately and completely upon the termination of the mandate regime, unless the Powers whose nationals were entitled on the 1st

9

August, 1914, to such rights should agree, or have agreed, by treaty to their suspension or modification.[14]

The U.S. now withdrew its objections to approval of the Palestine mandate and Lord Balfour, British delegate to the League Council, requested the Council on May 11 to place the Palestine draft mandate on the agenda for the nineteenth session, which was to begin on July 17, 1922.

In the meantime, Pope Benedict XV had died in January 1922, and Pius XI had come to the Papal throne on February 6, 1922. Pope Pius retained his predecessor's Secretary of State, Cardinal Gasparri, and the same policy on Palestine, but he applied the policy more vigorously than had his predecessor. The British Government, impatient at the delay in approving the Palestine draft mandate, had informed the League Council in January 1922 that it was ready to appoint the commission on the Holy Places and invited the Council to consider candidates for the presidency of the commission. Pope Pius sent the Latin Patriarch of Jerusalem, Monsignor Barlassina, to London to explain the Vatican's point of view on the mandate and the question of the Holy Places. Neither the Foreign Secretary, Lord Balfour, nor the Colonial Secretary, Winston Churchill, would receive him. The Vatican's views were therefore set forth in a letter written by Cardinal Gasparri to the Secretary General of the League of Nations on May 15, 1922.[15]

Cardinal Gasparri said in his letter that the Holy See was not opposed to the grant of the mandate over Palestine to Great Britain nor to the grant of equal rights in Palestine to Jews. On the other hand, the Vatican felt that the terms of the draft mandate gave the Jews a privileged position. As for Article 14, which provided for a commission to settle disputes over rights in the Holy Places, Cardinal Gasparri called it unacceptable. The Vatican felt that it was too vague as to the composition of the commission and it was therefore fearful of entrusting the question of Latin rights to such a body. The Vatican proposed that the commission be composed of the consuls in the Holy Land of those powers who were represented on the League Council.

Whatever may have been the intention or the expectations of the members of the British war cabinet that approved the

Balfour Declaration in 1917, it appears that after 1919 the British Government moved steadily away from any commitment to the ultimate establishment of a Jewish state or commonwealth in Palestine. Whether it was because the difficulties involved in implementing such a policy were too great or because the time was not yet right for such a prospect is not clear.[16] In any event, in June 1922 the British Government issued a statement in which it explained that the reason for inserting the provisions of the Balfour Declaration in the mandate was simply because "in order that this community should have the best prospect of free development and provide a full opportunity for the Jewish people to display its capacities, it is essential that it should know that it is in Palestine as of right and not on sufferance."[17] In reply to Cardinal Gasparri, the British Government wrote as follows to the Secretary General of the League of Nations on July 1, 1922: "The Council will observe that His Majesty's Government contemplate that the status of all citizens of Palestine in the eyes of the law shall be Palestinian, and that it has never been intended that they or any section of them should possess any other juridical status."[18]

In an effort to soothe Vatican apprehensions over Article 14, Great Britain also proposed on July 1, 1922, an alternative draft, which would have required the commission to submit its report to the League Council for confirmation. The new draft said:

> In order to determine the existing rights in the Holy Places and religious buildings or sites in Palestine which the mandatory is pledged under the preceding article to maintain, a commission consisting of not less than seven members shall be appointed by the mandatory, subject to the approval of the Council of the League of Nations. The duty of the commission shall be to frame a report defining these rights, including rights of ownership, user and access. The report shall be laid before the Council of the League of Nations for confirmation, and when confirmed shall be binding on the mandatory.
>
> In the preparation of their report the commission will consider all conflicting claims to any of the Holy Places and religious buildings or sites, and will endeavor in consultation with representatives of the confessions concerned to arrive at an agreed definition of existing rights. If no agreement can be

arrived at within a period to be fixed in each case by the commission, the commission after hearing all parties shall decide judicially on the claims of which it has had notice and shall embody such decisions in their report.

The report of the commission may also contain recommendations for ensuring that certain Holy Places, religious buildings or sites which the commission finds to be regarded with special veneration by the adherents of one particular religion are entrusted to the permanent control of suitable bodies representing the adherents of the religion concerned.

Such control will be guaranteed by the League of Nations.

The commission will settle its own procedure and shall appoint its own staff. Each member of the commission will in turn act as chairman of the commission. The expenses of the commission shall be defrayed by the League of Nations.

In all cases dealt with under this article, the right and duty of the mandatory to maintain order and decorum in the place concerned shall not be affected, and the buildings and sites will be subject to the provisions of such laws relating to the public monuments as may be enacted in Palestine with the approval of the mandatory.

Any religious confession which considers that the mandatory is not giving effect to the provisions of the report may appeal to the Council of the League who may require the mandatory to reassemble the commission for the purpose of considering and reporting upon any such appeal. Such report shall be laid before the Council of the League of Nations for confirmation, and when confirmed shall be binding on the mandatory.[19]

The draft mandate was discussed by the League Council in private session on July 22, 1922.[20] The Spanish delegate, Quiñones de Leon, who was President of the Council, informed the Council that the Papal Nuncio to France, Monsignor Ceretti, had been dispatched to London to explain the Vatican's views to the Council. Monsignor Ceretti was not invited to testify, but both the French delegate, René Viviani, and the Italian delegate, the Marquis Imperiali, raised questions concerning the new Article 14. They sought assurances that the majority of the commission would be Roman Catholics. In addition, Viviani said that Article 14 was contrary to Article 95 of the Treaty of Sèvres. As he understood the British proposal, Article 14 was intended to set up a provisional commission whose duty it would be to substitute a new regime for the status quo of 1852. In his view, Article 95 of the Treaty of

Sèvres called for a commission to adjudicate the rights of the various religious groups in the Holy Places and a small, provisional commission could not carry out this duty. The British delegate, Lord Balfour, denied that the British intended to substitute a new regime for the status quo, but he said that once the questions in contention were resolved, there would be no further need for the commission to sit. He insisted that the mandatory must be sovereign as stated in Article 13 and that the appointment of a permanent commission as a sort of executive power by the side of the mandatory power must be avoided. On the other hand, he saw no objection to having the commission meet whenever it appeared necessary. In the end, the Council revised Article 14 to read:

> A special commission shall be appointed by the mandatory to study and define the rights and claims in connection with the Holy Places and the rights and claims relating to the different religious communities in Palestine. The method of nomination, the composition and the functions of this commission shall be submitted to the Council of the League for its approval and the commission shall not be appointed or enter upon its functions until approved by the Council.[21]

Then the Spanish, French, Italian, and Belgian delegates each declared that his government considered it indispensable to have one of its citizens on the commission when it was constituted. The Council now approved the Palestine mandate and agreed that it should come into effect simultaneously with the mandate for Syria when the Italians and French reached agreement on Italian rights in Syria. This decision was confirmed at the public meeting of the Council on July 24, 1922.

The Holy Places Commission

On August 31, 1922, Lord Balfour submitted to the League Council a memorandom outlining a proposal for the commission on the Holy Places.[22] In essence, it provided for a commission divided into three sub-commissions, one Christian, one Muslim, and one Jewish. It was proposed that the Christian sub-commission be composed of a French president, three Roman Catholic representatives (Italian, Spanish, and Belgian), three Orthodox representatives (one of whom should

13

be Greek and one Russian), one Armenian, and one or possibly two representatives of the Abyssinians and the Copts. The Muslim sub-commission was to consist of an Italian president, a Palestinian Muslim, a French Muslim, and an Indian Muslim. The Jewish sub-commission was to consist of an American president, a Palestinian Jew, a British Jew, and a Portuguese (or Spanish) Jew to represent the Sephardis. The chairman of the whole commission was to be an American Protestant. According to the proposal, the duties of the commission were to be confined to settling claims or disputes and were not to include any administrative responsibilities. Where no unanimity could be achieved in a sub-commission, the question was to be referred to the chairman of the whole commission for decision.

The British proposal was discussed outside the League Council for almost five weeks. The Vatican called the proposal outrageous.[23] It objected that in the whole commission, the Christian members would be drowned in a majority composed of Muslims and Jews and that in the Christian sub-commission, the Latins would be outnumbered by Christians not in communion with Rome. In addition, the Vatican thought the American Protestant chairman of the whole commission would have undue power of decision. As an alternative, the French suggested three autonomous commissions: one Christian, one Muslim, and one Jewish.[24] The Christian commission would be divided into two sub-commissions: a four-man sub-commission for the Latins and a four-man sub-commission for the Orthodox and Armenians. The two Christian sub-commissions would meet separately on their own problems but they would meet jointly to consider matters that concerned both—for example, matters related to the Church of the Holy Sepulchre or the Church of the Nativity. In addition, the Christian commission would have a ninth Latin member who would be its president and would preside over joint meetings of the two sub-commissions. Thus, the Latins would be assured of a majority of one on the Christian commission. The French said that, of course, the presidency of the commission would be occupied by a Frenchman in view of France's historic role as protector of the Holy Places. The Italian delegate to the Council of the League of Nations, Marquis Imperiali, thought highly of the French proposal, but in view of the fact that the Latin Patriarch in Jerusalem was Italian, and in view of the fact that the preponderance of those who cared for the Holy Places had been Italian, the presidency of the commission should naturally go to an Italian.[25] A deadlock ensued.

In the meantime, with the demise of Russia as protecting power for the Orthodox, the British had come to assume that role in the Near East. This was evident in the close relations that had been developed between the Anglican Church and the Oecumenical Patriarchate,[26] particularly during the Greek venture in Anatolia from 1919 to 1922.[27] In Palestine, the British had come to see the advantage of protecting the Orthodox, especially at a time when the Vatican was lending encouragement to Muslim opposition to the mandate.[28] In addition, the Greek Government had been active immediately following the war in attempting to bring the Orthodox Patriarchate in Jerusalem under its protection, and the British were therefore desirous to preempt the position which the Greeks sought.

The Orthodox Patriarchate was heavily in debt at the close of the war as a result of the disappearance of its sources of revenue abroad, particularly in Russia. In addition, the Orthodox Church in Palestine was torn by a struggle between the Hellenizers and Arabizers. In the course of time, the Confraternity of the Holy Sepulchre had become almost entirely Greek, and since the members of the Holy Synod were appointed from the Confraternity, the Patriarchate itself had become Greek, while the laity and the parish clergy were Arabic-speaking Palestinians. During the latter part of the nineteenth century, the Arabs demanded a share in the administration of the affairs of the Patriarchate, and trouble broke out in 1872 and 1908. Taking advantage of the financial troubles of the Patriarchate, the Greek Government in September 1919 offered to give the Patriarchate a monthly subsidy through the National Bank of Greece, provided that the Patriarchate accept a new set of internal regulations drawn up in Athens by two Greek prelates and two members of the Greek Foreign Office.[29]

The Holy Synod was disposed to accept the Greek proposal at once, but the Patriarch and the Arabizers were opposed, since the new regulations would have made the Patriarchate a dependency of the Greek Government. The Holy Synod attempted to depose the Patriarch, but the Mandatory Government intervened in January 1921 by appointing a commission of inquiry, the Bertram-Luke Commission, to determine what measures should be taken to restore order in the affairs of the Patriarchate and to liquidate its debts. In accordance with the recommendations of the Bertram-Luke Commission, a second commission was appointed in August 1921 to manage the finances of the Patriarchate.[30] The debt situation was resolved without recourse to the Greek loan and peace was temporarily restored in the Patriarchate.

It was against this background that Lord Balfour addressed himself to the matter of the Holy Places commission in the Council of the League of Nations on October 4, 1922.[31] He said that Great Britain was in no position to settle a dispute between the Catholic powers over the presidency of the Christian commission and that before any further progress could be made on the appointment of the Holy Places commission, the Catholic powers would have to resolve their own differences. He then noted that there were no Orthodox powers on the League Council. Great Britain, as the mandatory, was responsible for seeing that all the religious groups in Palestine, including the Orthodox, were dealt with fairly. Therefore, no scheme could be accepted that did not guarantee justice for the Orthodox.

The differences between Italy and France on the question of the Holy Places commission were never resolved. In fact, their differences over Italian rights in Syria also continued to be unresolved, and the British delegate, impatient at the Council's delay in allowing the implementation of the already approved mandate instrument for Palestine, raised the matter in the League Council again on September 28, 1923. He suggested that the Council drop its insistence on the simultaneous implementation of the Syrian and Palestinian mandates and agree to allowing the mandate to take effect simultaneously with the Treaty of Lausanne. The French and Italians thereupon settled their differences on Syria, announcing it the following day. Thus, the Syrian and Palestinian mandates became effective on September 29, 1923. However, the Spanish delegate noted for the record that the question of the application of Article 14 was still reserved.[32]

The Status Quo Maintained

In the absence of agreement on the implementation of Article 14, the responsibility for settling difficulties and disputes in the Holy Places devolved entirely upon the mandatory. Consequently in 1924 an order in council was published which withdrew from the law courts of Palestine any case in connection with rights and claims in the Holy Places and vested jurisdiction in such cases in the British High Commissioner.[33] According to the order in council, the High Commissioner's decisions were final and binding on all parties.

The question of implementing Article 14 of the mandate came up again in late 1929 and early 1930. Disturbances over the Wailing Wall broke out in August 1929, and the British Government proposed to the Permanent Mandates Commission of the League of Nations on November 18, 1929, the appointment under Article 14 of an ad hoc commission to settle the question of Jewish and Muslim rights and claims to the Wailing Wall.[34] The Permanent Mandates Commission concluded that the appointment of an ad hoc commission to deal with only one of the Holy Places was not in conformity with Article 14, which called for a special commission to deal with all of the Holy Places.[35] The matter was then referred to the Council of the League, where the British delegate said that the U.K. was willing to proceed with the appointment of the special commission provided for by Article 14, and to limit its duties for the time being to the problem of the Wailing Wall.[36] However, the Council decided on January 14, 1930, to continue to leave Article 14 unimplemented and to authorize the appointment of an ad hoc commission under Article 13.*

*League of Nations, *Official Journal*, February 1930, pp. 92-93. The Wailing Wall Commission was appointed in May 1930. The Commission's report, published in December 1930, concluded that the Muslims had the sole proprietary rights to the Wailing Wall and the pavement in front of the Wall. On the other hand, the Jews had the right of free access to the Wailing Wall at all times for the purpose of devotions. But strict limitations were imposed on bringing religious appurtenances to the Wall, and the blowing of the ram's horn (*shofar*) was forbidden. See International Commission for the Wailing Wall, *Report of the Commission . . . to Determine the Rights and Claims of Moslems and Jews in Connection with the Western or Wailing Wall at Jerusalem.*

In the realm of Orthodox affairs, the dispute between the Hellenizers and Arabizers broke into the open again in August 1922 when the Holy Synod in Jerusalem elected a metropolitan for Nazareth who could not speak Arabic. According to the Ottoman Imperial Regulations of 1875, the metropolitans in Acre and in Nazareth were required to be acquainted with Arabic.[37] In March of 1925 the Mandatory Government appointed a commission, the Bertram-Young Commission, to look into the whole question of the Patriarchate's relations with the Orthodox community in Palestine and to recommend what steps should be taken to amend the Regulations of 1875 to bring about a more harmonious relationship. The Commission recommended in June 1925 that the election of the pastoral metropolitans should be made subject, like the election of the Patriarch, to recognition by the Mandatory Government.[38] The Commission also produced a draft ordinance that would do three things: permit the local community a greater voice in the conduct of the financial affairs of the Patriarchate; broaden the composition of the Holy Synod to include all metropolitans and bishops subject to the Patriarch; and require that the members of the Confraternity of the Holy Sepulchre, and hence the Holy Synod, be Palestinian citizens.[39] The Commission admitted that this third requirement was not designed so much to guarantee admission of Arabs to the Confraternity as it was to assure that the Confraternity, the Synod, and the Patriarch not become subject to a foreign power (that is, Greece).[40] These recommendations were not immediately enacted into law, and the dispute broke out again in 1931 over who was to succeed the Patriarch Damianos, who died on August 14, 1931. Timotheos was elected in July 1935, but the Arabs objected.[41] It was not until 1938 that a compromise was worked out under which most of the principles of the Bertram-Young report were to be implemented. The British extended official recognition to Patriarch Timotheos in October 1939.[42] And in November 1941, the Ottoman Imperial Regulations of 1875 were replaced by a new ordinance on the organization and administration of the Patriarchate.[43]

Thus, in the arrangements made for Palestine following World War I, the Catholic powers acquiesced in a situation not consonant with their desires but at least not unsatisfactory to them. Control of Jerusalem and the Holy Places went with control of Palestine, and British control in their view was better than Turkish control. If they had been unable to improve the position of the Latins in the Holy Places, they had at least prevented it from deteriorating further. The Orthodox were satisfied with British control of Jerusalem and Bethlehem as long as the status quo of 1852 was adhered to. Since Jerusalem was in the hands of a Protestant power, Protestants found little of a religious nature to complain about. With the Balfour Declaration incorporated in the mandate, the Zionists were happy enough to have Jerusalem in British hands, at least while the Jews were still in a minority in Palestine. The Arabs, upset by both the Balfour Declaration and the whole idea of the mandate, were the most unhappy of all and they refused to cooperate in any large measure with the British. They feared that in the course of time the Jews would become a majority and that the British would give the Jews self-government throughout Palestine and then disappear. But the large-scale Jewish immigration that had been forecast did not materialize in the 1920's, and Arab grievances did not reach crisis proportions until the mid-1930's.

The interest of the United States in Palestine during this period was limited. President Wilson had shown some interest in the country at the Paris Peace Conference as part of the larger problem of what to do with the Arab portions of the Ottoman Empire, and it was due in large part to his efforts that the system of mandates suggested by South Africa's General Smuts was adopted for dealing with the problem. He was also instrumental in getting the Supreme Council to agree on March 23, 1919, to send an inter-allied commission to the Near East to study and report on the wishes of the area's inhabitants. In the end, only the American members of the commission, Charles R. Crane and Henry C. King, went on the mission. The King-Crane Commission filed its report with the American delegation to the Peace Conference on August 28, 1919. The report recommended, among other things, that Palestine be included in a united Syrian state under Amir Faysal, son of the Sharif of Mecca, and that this state be placed under a single mandatory, preferably the United States or Great Britain. The Commission also recommended that the Holy Places be cared for by an international and inter-religious commission under the oversight and approval of the mandatory and the League of Nations. By the time the report was filed, however, President Wilson had returned to the United States. American attention was now absorbed by the debate in the Senate over the Treaty of Versailles, and the King-Crane report, being unfavorable to French and British plans for the area, was quietly pigeonholed.

With the Senate's rejection of the Treaty of Versailles and the defeat of the Democrats in the presidential election of 1920, American foreign policy returned to its prewar isolationism. In the Near East, American policy was directed toward assuring the rights of American citizens and protecting American commercial interests, missionary efforts, and philanthropic endeavors. It was to accomplish these purposes that the Anglo-American Treaty of 1924 was negotiated under the Harding Administration. In return for U.S. recognition of the British mandate over Palestine, the treaty guaranteed to Americans equality of treatment in Palestine with the nationals of the members of the League of Nations. Once the Anglo-American Treaty was ratified, the United States considered its interests in Jerusalem and Palestine to be adequately protected. Americans were content to let the British worry about the details of administering Jerusalem and safeguarding the Holy Places for the world at large.

Chapter 2

Jerusalem and the Arab-Jewish Problem

The Royal Commission of 1937

By 1936 the question of Palestine was no longer primarily a European problem, for it was now caught up in an intense struggle between two nationalisms: Zionism and Palestinian Arab nationalism. Nevertheless, the European powers still had interests there, particularly in Jerusalem. This was to lead to proposals, advanced for the first time in 1937, for a separate regime for Jerusalem in order to remove it as a prize for the victor in the struggle for Palestine.

Hitler's rise to power in Germany in 1933 had spurred Jewish emigration to Palestine. While it is difficult to obtain reliable statistics on the composition of the pre-World War I population of Palestine, the Jewish population was estimated to be about 12.3 per cent of the total population of the country in 1914.[1] There was considerable displacement of population during the war, and when a census was taken in 1922, it was found that Jews constituted 11.1 per cent of the total. The Jewish population had increased by June 30, 1933, to only 18.9 per cent of the total. But within the next three years, it had jumped to 27.7 per cent. It looked as though the large-scale Jewish immigration that had been expected in the 1920's was at last beginning to materialize.

On the other hand, nationalism had grown to a potent force in the Arab world and nationalist demonstrations and strikes in Syria and Egypt had produced assurances in London and Paris by March 1936 that treaties would be concluded recognizing the independence of those two countries. Further, Palestine's neighboring Arab states began about 1936 to take an active interest in Palestinian affairs. The mandatory power found it increasingly difficult to maintain peace between the Arabs and Jews in Palestine, and in 1936 widespread disorder broke out. It soon took the form of an Arab uprising under the direction of the Arab Higher Committee formed on April 25, 1936, under the presidency of Hajj Amin al-Husayni, the Mufti of Jerusalem. Mayor Husayn al-Khalidi of Jerusalem, an Arab Muslim, joined the Arab Higher Committee, and the Municipal Government, a mixed body of Arabs and Jews, was virtually out of operation. Through appeals from the leaders of the surrounding Arab states, order was eventually restored and a Royal Commission headed by Earl Peel (William Robert Wellesley), former Secretary of State for India, was dispatched to survey the situation and to recommend a solution.

The Royal Commission heard testimony from November 1936 until February 1937, both in Palestine and in London. The Arabs strongly criticized the Balfour Declaration and expressed the fear that the Jews would soon become a majority and that the mandatory power would then turn the country over to them. They professed to believe that, once the Jews became a majority, the Haram al-Sharif would be destroyed and the Jewish temple rebuilt.[2] The solution of the problem, according to the Arabs, lay in abandonment of the experiment of the Jewish national home, the immediate stoppage of Jewish immigration, the immediate prohibition of the sale of Arab land to Jews, and replacement of the mandate by a treaty between Great Britain and Palestine along the lines of the British-Iraqi treaty.

The representatives of the Jewish Agency told the Royal Commission that the mandate should be interpreted in accordance with full Jewish claims: there must be no new restrictions on the sale of Arab land to Jews; there must be no restriction on immigration other than that imposed by the economic absorptive capacity of the country; no measures must be taken to prevent the Jewish population from becoming in due course a majority in Palestine; and "if and when it becomes a majority, no veto should be put on Palestine becoming a Jewish State, in the sense that the Jews would have a major voice in its government."[3]

The Jews were prepared, however, to make a concession on the last point.[4] They said that they did not want to dominate an Arab minority any more than they wished to be dominated by an Arab majority. They were therefore prepared to agree that if a legislative council were immediately established and if the current Jewish minority were given a number of seats in it equal to the number held by Arabs, they would never claim more than parity whatever the future ratio between the Jewish and Arab populations might become.

The Royal Commission reasoned that parity would undoubtedly be rejected by the Arabs, since it implied what they refused to admit—the potential right of the Jews to an equal share with them in the government.[5] The Commission also decided that transformation of Palestine into a unitary state with representative government based on the population as it then stood was not feasible since the population was not sufficiently homogeneous so as "to enable the minority to acquiesce in the rule of the majority and to make it possible for the balance of power to readjust itself from time to time."[6] Yet the Royal Commission recognized that the Arabs in Palestine were as fit to govern themselves as the Arabs of Iraq or Syria and that the Jews were as fit to govern themselves as any organized and educated community in Europe or elsewhere. In the Commission's view, conditions under the mandate would continue to deteriorate, since both the Arabs and the Jews were highly nationalistic and this nationalism was being fed to the youth in the school systems.

The Commission therefore concluded that the mandate was unworkable, and it recommended that Palestine be partitioned. In this connection, the Royal Commission reviewed the policy statements of the British Government on Palestine through 1922 and it decided that while there had been no definite commitment to establish a Jewish state in Palestine, there had been no prohibition against the ultimate establishment of such a state.[7]

The Royal Commission's Plan

The Royal Commission's plan called for: a permanent British mandatory zone including Jerusalem, Bethlehem, and a narrow corridor to the sea at Jaffa; a sovereign Jewish state embracing the Galilee and the coastal plain as far south as Ashdod; and a sovereign Arab state to include Jaffa and the rest of Palestine and Transjordan. It was also recommended that Nazareth and Lake Tiberias be covered by the mandate as well. The Commission specified that all those domiciled in the mandatory zone would retain the status of British-protected persons, while the remainder of the Palestinian population would become citizens of either the Jewish state or the

Arab state. The reasoning of the Royal Commission in recommending a permanent separate regime for Jerusalem was set forth in its conclusions:

> The partition of Palestine is subject to the overriding necessity of keeping the sanctity of Jerusalem and Bethlehem inviolate and of ensuring free and safe access to them for all the world. That, in the fullest sense of the mandatory phrase, is "a sacred trust of civilization"—a trust on behalf not merely of the peoples of Palestine but of multitudes in other lands to whom these places, one or both, are Holy Places....
>
> We regard the protection of the Holy Places as a permanent trust, unique in its character and purpose.... We submit for consideration that, in order to avoid misunderstanding, it might frankly be stated that this trust will only terminate if and when the League of Nations and the United States desire it to do so, and that, while it would be the trustee's duty to promote the well-being and development of the local population concerned, it is not intended that in the course of time they should stand by themselves as a wholly self-governing community.[8]

The Royal Commission's report was published on July 7, 1937, and a statement of policy was published simultaneously by the Secretary of State for the Colonies.[9] The statement of policy whole-heartedly endorsed the Royal Commission's report and said that the British Government would take the necessary steps for implementing the proposed solution. The report and the statement of policy were debated in the House of Lords on July 20-21 and in the House of Commons on July 21. The House of Commons approved a motion that the partition proposal be brought before the League of Nations "with a view to enabling His Majesty's Government, after adequate inquiry, to present to Parliament a definite scheme."[10]

The Permanent Mandates Commission of the League of Nations took up the matter on July 30 and was none too enthusiastic about the Royal Commission's report. In general, the Mandates Commission felt that the British were attempting to dodge the responsibility laid upon them by the mandate to develop the Jewish national home in Palestine. After a prolonged examination, the Permanent Mandates Commission expressed the view that "the present Mandate became almost unworkable once it was publicly declared so by a British Royal Commission."[11] The Permanent Mandates Commission therefore reported to the League Council that it had concluded that it was worth continuing the examination of the partition scheme. However, the Commission recommended that in the event of partition the two states should not become sovereign immediately but should remain under mandate for a while longer. When the Mandates Commission's report was discussed by the League Council on September 14, 1937, the French delegate, Yvon Delbos, probably mindful of France's difficulties in Syria, was sympathetic to Britain's difficulties in Palestine. He was probably also concerned about the effect on Syria of French endorsement of partition in Palestine. Consequently, he expressed French approval of the search for a solution in Palestine but reserved France's position on the substance of the solution.

Neither the League Council nor the Permanent Mandates Commission found any difficulty with the British proposal to retain a British mandate over Jerusalem. The British delegate, Anthony Eden, was careful to explain that the U.K. was not giving up the trust which it exercised on behalf of the world in the Holy Places. He said:

> His Majesty's Government . . . concluded, from the terms of Article 28 of the existing mandate, that it was the intention and wish of the League that the holy places, including the Christian holy places, should remain permanently under League supervision and control. The vast majority of the Christian holy places were in the three cities of Jerusalem, Bethlehem, and Nazareth. The two latter were almost entirely Christian towns. In the old city of Jerusalem and its immediate environs were not only many historic religious sites but the religious settlements of many faiths. The United Kingdom Government thought it would be in accordance with the wishes of the vast majority of States Members of the League that, when contemplating the ultimate establishment of Jewish and Arab States in the Holy Land sacred to all three religions, those religious sites and institutions should be placed permanently in the case of a Power acting on behalf of and responsible to the League as a whole for what must always be a sacred trust.[12]

The Chairman of the Permanent Mandates Commission, also appearing before the League Council, said that the

Commission approved of the proposal of the British Royal Commission that "the holy places should not be under the sovereignty of either of the proposed new States."[13] The League Council approved the Mandates Commission's report.

Reaction to the Partition Plan

In the meantime, Transjordanian Amir Abdallah reportedly accepted the partition proposal, although he did not say so publicly.[14] For him, it offered certain advantages. When he had arrived in Amman in February 1921, he was on his way to Damascus with a force of Hijazis to recover the throne from which his brother, Faysal, had been driven by the French in 1920. Wishing to avoid difficulty with the French, the British persuaded him to relinquish in favor of Faysal the throne of Iraq, for which he himself had been destined, and to accept instead an amirate in Palestine east of the Jordan River, where they were having difficulty in establishing order. Accordingly, the application of the Jewish national home provisions were suspended in Transjordan under Article 25 of the mandate and a separate administration was established there under Amir Abdallah.* In accepting this arrangement, Abdallah regarded Amman only as a temporary stopping place on the road to Damascus and the throne of a unified Syria in which he hoped to include the Lebanon and Palestine, as well as Transjordan. The partition scheme put forth by the Royal Commission meant that Abdallah would not only acquire a larger kingdom and part of the territory which he hoped to include anyway but would also acquire greater resources, both human and material, with which to pursue his Greater Syria scheme.

*As already pointed out, the British interpreted the pledge made by Sir Henry McMahon to Sharif Husayn as excluding Cisjordan but including Transjordan in the independent Arab state. In accordance with this interpretation, Article 25 of the Palestine mandate instrument provided that the mandatory could suspend, with the consent of the Council of the League of Nations, such provisions as it considered "inapplicable to local conditions" in those territories of Palestine lying east of the Jordan. The suspension was officially notified to the League Council on September 16, 1922. The Council gave its approval the same day. See Great Britain, Parliamentary Papers, Cmd. 5479, Chapter II, para. 41, and Appendix 1.

The other Arabs were indignant over the Royal Commission's partition proposal. Hajj Amin al-Husayni, the Mufti of Jerusalem and Chairman of the Arab Higher Committee, opposed it vigorously. The Prime Minister of Iraq, in a statement to the press, called on all Arabs to defend the rights of the Palestinian Arabs. A non-governmental Pan-Arab Congress met at Bludan, Syria, and on September 10, 1937, rejected the partition plan, called for immediate Palestinian independence with an Arab government, and criticized Amir Abdallah for his readiness to acquiesce in the partition proposal.

The Jews received the report of the Royal Commission with mixed feelings. Many of them, such as Menachem Ussishkin, opposed it because it offered too little; they wanted a Jewish state that would include all of Palestine, and they opposed partition and termination of the mandate until this objective was assured. The extreme Orthodox Jews opposed partition on religious grounds, believing that restoration of the state was the work of the Messiah and should not be presumptuously undertaken by ordinary Jews. Many non-Zionist Jews, particularly in the U.S., opposed it because they felt the creation of a Jewish state would call into question, at least in the minds of non-Jews, their loyalty to the countries of which they were citizens. The Marxist-oriented Hashomer Hatzair believed that the Arab-Jewish conflict was an issue invented by the bourgeoisie and that the partition proposal only served to detract from what it regarded as the more fundamental, trans-nationalist issue—that is, the class struggle. On the other hand, many, like Dr. Chaim Weizmann, believed that the immediate creation of a Jewish state, although not as large as the Jews would like, would be preferable to continuation of the mandate under the alternative proposals of the Royal Commission. At least, a Jewish state would be able to control its own immigration policies, whereas the Peel Commission had recommended restrictions on Jewish immigration if the mandate was to continue.

The partition proposal was debated at length in the Twentieth Zionist Congress, which met in Zurich in August 1937. The resolution adopted by the congress represented a compromise between the supporters and the opponents of partition. The congress rejected the scheme of partition put forth by the Royal Commission, but it empowered the executive of the Zionist organization to negotiate with the British Government "with a view to ascertaining the precise terms of His Majesty's Government for the proposed establishment of a Jewish state."[15] However, the executive was not empowered to commit itself or the Zionist organization to any precise scheme but was to refer any scheme that might emerge to a new congress for its decision.

But authority for dealing with the British Government, which had been granted to the Zionist organization by the mandate instrument, had been transferred in 1929, with British approval, to the Jewish Agency. Meeting in Zurich immediately after the Twentieth Zionist Congress, the Jewish Agency considered the resolutions of the congress but decided to direct the Agency executive to request the British Government to convene a conference of Palestinian Jews and Palestinian Arabs to explore the possibilities of a settlement "for an undivided Palestine on the basis of the Balfour Declaration and the Mandate."[16] It was also decided that if such a conference did not materialize, the powers of negotiation for a settlement by partition would be transferred from the executive of the Zionist organization to the executive of the Jewish Agency and the final authority for deciding on the acceptability of any such scheme would be transferred from the Zionist Congress to the Council of the Jewish Agency.

In October 1937 Colonial Secretary Ormsby-Gore rejected the idea of a conference of Palestinian Arabs and Jews as impracticable. The Jewish Agency then put forth a proposal providing for a Jewish state that would include the coastal plain between Migdal and Hadera (except for Jaffa, which would be included in the Arab state), all of Palestine north of Jenin, both sides of the Jordan Valley in Palestine and Transjordan between Lake Tiberias and Tirat Zvi, and a corridor to Jerusalem. The Arab state would include the rest of Transjordan, the West Bank north of Ramallah and Jericho and an area including Khan Yunis (but not Rafah), Beersheba, Beit Guvrin, Migdal, and Gaza. The British mandatory zone would include the Negev south of Beersheba, the west bank of the Dead Sea, Hebron, Bethlehem, Jericho, Ramallah, and a corridor to the sea at Jaffa. Jerusalem would be divided between the Jewish state and the mandatory zone, with Mount Scopus and the modern western sections outside the walls going to the Jewish state and with the Walled City and the area east of the walls to the mandatory zone.

In justifying the proposals on Jerusalem, the Jewish memorandum acknowledged the necessity of entrusting the Holy Places to the custody of the mandatory power as an international trustee, but it pointed out that the Holy Places are concentrated in the Walled City and that

> ...the need of a special regime for that part of the town cannot justify the exclusion of the whole of Jerusalem from the Jewish State. It has been truly said that Jewish Palestine without Jerusalem would be a body without a soul. Jerusalem has throughout the ages been the spiritual center of the Jews, dispersed as they were over the face of the earth. . . . It is a symbol of Jewish national life and practically synonymous in the minds of Jews with Palestine. Throughout the ages, Jews have persisted, in spite of all obstacles, in attempting to reestablish themselves in Jerusalem. In this latest phase of the Return to Zion, Jews have built the greater part of the new Jerusalem outside the city walls. . . . The separation of this Jerusalem from the Jewish State is an injustice to both. Apart from the special significance of Jerusalem, spiritual and political, the loss thereby entailed to the Jewish State in terms of population, economic position, and taxable capacity would be irreparable.[17]

Official U.S. interest in the report of the Royal Commission did not run very deep. The stand of the Roosevelt administration was consistent with the Palestine policy it had inherited from the Republican administrations of the 1920's. The State Department was desirous of making certain that American rights and interests were not affected. In the U.S. view, the U.S. had the right under Article 7 of the Anglo-American Treaty of 1924 to be consulted on any proposed modifications of the mandate.* A series of exchanges on this point took

*Article 7 stipulated that American rights would not be "affected by any modification which may be made in the terms of the Mandate . . . unless such modifications shall have been assented to by the United States." (Text of the treaty found in United States, Department of State, *Mandate for Palestine*, pp. 107-14.) Prior to World War II, the U.S. interpreted Article 7 narrowly. Following World War II, Article 7 was much more broadly interpreted. Since Transjordan, for example, constituted part of the Palestine mandate, Article 7 became the basis for U.S. official interest in the political development of Jordan in 1946-48.

place in London in 1937 between the American ambassador and the British Government.[18] In the end, however, the U.S. could not prevent modifications of the mandate. A public memorandum issued by the State Department on October 14, 1938, said:

> It is expected...that this Government will have an opportunity to submit its views to the British Government with respect to any changes affecting American rights which may be proposed in the Palestine Mandate. These rights, which are defined by the American-British Convention or Treaty of December 3, 1924, comprise nondiscriminatory treatment in matters of commerce; non-impairment of vested American property rights; permission for American nationals to establish and maintain educational, philanthropic, and religious institutions in Palestine; safeguards with respect to the judiciary; and, in general, equality of treatment with all other foreign nationals.
>
> The rights of the United States in connection with any changes in terms of the Palestine Mandate are set forth in article 7 of the above-mentioned treaty....
>
> This article is substantially identical with corresponding articles included in eight other existing agreements concluded by this Government with respect to the mandated territories.... None of these articles empower the Government of the United States to prevent the modification of the terms of any of the mandates. Under their provisions, however, this Government can decline to recognize the validity of the application to American interests of any modification of the mandates unless such modification has been assented to by the Government of the United States.[19]

President Roosevelt took the same position five days later in a letter to Senator Millard Tydings.[20]

The Abandonment of Partition

After considerable delay, the British Government appointed in March 1938 a new commission, the Palestine Partition Commission, headed by Sir John Woodhead, to elaborate the Royal Commission's partition plan. The report of the Palestine Partition Commission was published in October 1938.[21] It elaborated three partition proposals. Plan A was, with slight modifications, the one recommended by the Peel Commission. Plan B called for a Jewish state along the lines of the Peel proposals, but without the Galilee and the area south of Wadi Rubin; the Galilee would be mandated territory like the Jerusalem enclave and the rest of the country would be included in the Arab state. Plan C confined the Jewish state to the coastal plain between Tantura and Wadi Rubin, minus Jaffa and the Jerusalem corridor. The coastal plain north of Tantura, the Galilee, and the Jordan Valley would constitute a northern mandated territory. The Negev and Rafah would constitute a southern mandated territory. The rest of the country, minus the Jerusalem enclave, would be included in the Arab state.

The boundaries of the Jerusalem mandatory zone were identical in all three plans and provided for a larger enclave than did the Peel Commission. The Partition Commission included Ramallah because of the broadcasting station, Aqir in order to provide space for a first-class airfield for the Royal Air Force, and a wider corridor between Ramla and the coast in order to provide a more secure access to the sea. The Commission made clear that the proposal for an enlarged enclave was based on defense "and that if the Mandatory is to be entrusted with the protection of the Holy Places, it is essential that the Enclave should have boundaries which are capable of being defended."[22]

The Commission rejected the Jewish proposal that Mount Scopus and the western part of Jerusalem outside the walls be included in the Jewish state, reasoning that both the Muslim and Christian worlds would oppose the inclusion of any part of Jerusalem in the Jewish state, and that in any case division of the city would impose serious, even if not insurmountable, administrative problems.

Having outlined its three partition plans, the Commission concluded its report by recommending against partition.[23] Plans A and B, they said, would leave large numbers of Arabs within the Jewish state, roughly 50 per cent under Plan A and 38 per cent under Plan B. The Commission concluded that this problem could not be solved by population exchange, since there would not be enough Jews in the Arab state to transfer. Hence, neither Plan A nor Plan B would lead to peace. The Commission rejected the Jewish partition proposal on the same grounds. As for Plan C, the Commission did not believe the Arab and Jewish states thus created could be economically viable.

The British were particularly desirous now of seeing tranquility restored to Palestine. War clouds were already gathering in Europe, and in the event of war it would be absolutely essential that there be no threat to British security along the vital sea route to India and Australia. This meant, above all, reaching an accommodation with Arab nationalism. A conference of Arabs and Jews was now proposed. The conference took place in London in February and March of 1939 in the form of parallel talks between the British and an Arab delegation on the one side and the British and a Jewish delegation on the other, but no settlement was forthcoming. The British Government therefore decided to proceed with a solution of its own, and the sessions with the Arabs and Jews were terminated on March 17.

The new British policy was set forth in the White Paper of May 17, 1939.[24] The White Paper again rejected the view that the McMahon correspondence with Sharif Husayn did not exclude Palestine west of the Jordan from the proposed Arab state. It also confirmed the British obligation under the mandate to facilitate the establishment of a national home for the Jews in Palestine, but the White Paper said that the British Government saw nothing in the mandate instrument or previous statements of policy that required it to transform Palestine into a Jewish state against the will of the Arab inhabitants. The White Paper acknowledged that in earlier statements of policy the British Government had interpreted its obligations under the national home provisions of the mandate to mean that Jewish immigration into Palestine should be permitted in accordance with the economic capacity of the country to absorb new arrivals. On the other hand, the White Paper said that the British Government saw nothing in the mandate instrument or former statements of policy that required it to permit Jewish immigration to continue indefinitely and without regard to other than economic conditions. The White Paper said that indefinite immigration would only produce more strife in Palestine. Further, the White Paper contended that the national home had now been established and the commitments to this end had therefore been fulfilled. Hence, the new policy envisaged the establishment within ten years of an independent Palestinian state in treaty relationship with Great Britain. In the new state, Jews and Arabs would jointly exercise governmental authority. In the mean-time, Jewish immigration was restricted to an additional 75,000 unless the Arabs consented to further immigration, and the transfer of Arab land to Jews would be restricted. The White Paper also specified that in the constitution of Palestine or in the treaty to be concluded between Palestine and Great Britain, provisions would have to be included to assure the security of, and freedom of access to, the Holy Places and the protection of the interests of the various religious bodies.

The Permanent Mandates Commission examined the White Paper of 1939 at length from June 15 through June 28, 1939.[25] In its observations reported to the League Council, the Mandates Commission concluded that the policy set out in the White Paper was not in accordance with the interpretation which, in agreement with the mandatory power and the League Council, the Mandates Commission had always placed on the Palestine mandate.[26] Three of the members of the Commission (the British, French, and Portuguese members) believed, however, that in the circumstances, the policy of the White Paper was justified and that the mandate might therefore be reinterpreted provided the League Council did not oppose it. The other four members (the Belgian, Swiss, Dutch, and Norwegian members) felt that the mandate might not be reinterpreted in this fashion.* One member noted that after all the battles fought through the centuries to establish Christian rule in Palestine because of the Holy Places, the mandatory power was embarking on a policy that would mean abandonment of Christian control of the Holy Places and handing them over to two non-Christian peoples. All the members of the Commission agreed that the considerations put forward in the report of the Royal Commission in 1937 and in the preliminary opinion presented to the League Council by the Mandates Commission on the Royal Commission report were still relevant and that partition should be borne in mind at the appropriate moment.

The Mayoralty Problem in Jerusalem

The outbreak of war in Europe in September 1939 brought Great Britain a brief respite in Palestine. Although the Jews

*The seats of the Spanish, German, Italian, and Japanese members were vacant.

were unhappy with the White Paper of 1939, they were nevertheless completely committed to the Allied cause against Nazi Germany. The White Paper, the presence of large numbers of Allied troops, the eventual decline in Axis fortunes, unparalleled economic prosperity, and disunity in the Palestinian Arab nationalist movement served to keep the Arabs relatively quiet during the war. However, by 1944, there were already signs of what was to come after the war.

The most significant portent was perhaps the Arab-Jewish struggle for the mayoralty of Jerusalem following the death of Mayor Mustafa Bey al-Khalidi on August 24, 1944. The Jerusalem Municipality was administered by a municipal council consisting of six Arabs and six Jews elected in accordance with the provisions of the Municipal Corporations Ordinance of 1934, and a mayor and two deputy mayors appointed by the High Commissioner from among the members of the Municipal Council. The mayor had always been a Muslim since the formation of the Municipality in 1877, and the deputy mayors appointed by the High Commissioner were Christian and Jewish. But the Muslims had never constituted a majority of the population of the Municipality of Jerusalem (see Appendix A). In fact, as late as 1922, when the mandatory power took the first census in Palestine, Christians outnumbered Muslims, and Jews outnumbered both. It is difficult to know exactly when the Jews became the majority in Jerusalem. American consular officers in Jerusalem during the first ten years of the Municipality, from 1877 until 1887, consistently reported the population of Jerusalem to be composed of 50 per cent Jews, 25 per cent Christians, and 25 per cent Muslims.[27] After the pogroms of 1887 in Russia, Jews began to migrate to Palestine in numbers, and many of these came to Jerusalem. By 1905 Jerusalem's population was estimated to be 60,000 of which 66.6 per cent were Jews (see Appendix A). There was a considerable displacement of Jews during World War I, but the census in 1922 showed that Jews still constituted 54.3 per cent of the population of Jerusalem. By 1944 the proportion of Jews had reached 60.6 per cent of the total population of Jerusalem, while Muslims constituted 21.1 per cent and Christians 18.3 per cent of the total.

Thus, when Mayor Khalidi died, the Jewish Agency demanded that the High Commissioner appoint a Jew as mayor.

The Muslims contested the Jewish demand on the grounds that the succession of Muslim mayors since the formation of the Municipality had established a binding precedent. Further, they pointed to the fact that Jerusalem was one of the Holy Cities of Islam, and that except for a period during the Crusades it had been administered by Muslims in one form or another since its capture in the days of the Caliph Umar in A.D. 638.

The British High Commissioner had the authority under the Municipal Corporations Ordinance of 1934 and the Defense Regulations of 1938 to fill the Council vacancy caused by Khalidi's death by either election or appointment. He hesitated to do this, however, until the mayoralty dispute was settled. Under the temporary arrangement following Mayor Khalidi's death, the Jewish Deputy Mayor, Daniel Auster, was Acting Mayor and the Jews constituted a majority on the Council. The temporary arrangement being advantageous to the Jews, the High Commissioner knew that they were prepared to live with it indefinitely. On the other hand, the Commissioner knew that if Arab strength on the Council were brought back up to 50 per cent before the dispute was settled, a stalemate would develop. Consequently, on March 21, 1945, he submitted a proposal that would have reduced both the Arabs and Jews to a minority on the Council. The proposal was to fill the Arab vacancy by the appointment of a Muslim councillor and to appoint two additional councillors who would be British. The Municipal Council was invited to agree to annual rotation of the mayoralty to Muslim, Christian, and Jewish councillors, with the understanding that the Christian mayor need not be Palestinian. The Arabs rejected the plan and a one-day general strike was called on March 24 as a protest to the High Commissioner's proposal. The Jews agreed on March 23 to accept it, provided that the mayoralty term be two years instead of one, that the first mayor under the plan be Jewish, and that the third mayor be British.

Following their rejection of the British High Commissioner's plan, the Arab councillors boycotted the meetings of the Municipal Council. Under the Municipal Corporations Ordinance, councillors were disqualified to sit as councillors after three months of consecutive absences. The Arab seats thus became vacant upon the expiration of the specified period, and it was no longer possible to obtain a legal quorum for doing business. The British High Commissioner therefore authorized the District Commissioner of Jerusalem to appoint a commission of six British officials to continue the administration of Jerusalem. This commission was appointed on July 11, 1945, and it lasted until the end of the mandatory regime.

The High Commissioner also appointed Sir William Fitz-Gerald, the Chief Justice, to inquire into the local administration of Jerusalem and to recommend a solution to the crisis. FitzGerald made his report on August 30, 1945, and recommended that the Walled City be placed under a British administrative council and that the rest of Jerusalem be divided into two autonomous boroughs, one Arab and one Jewish. But by the time FitzGerald submitted his report World War II had ended, and the whole Palestine issue had come to the fore again. Consequently, the report was quietly shelved. Jerusalem was caught up in the Arab-Jewish struggle.

Chapter 3

The Trip to Limbo

The British Failure

With the liberation of the inmates of the Nazi death camps at the end of World War II, the Palestine problem once again assumed crisis proportions. Under the terms of the White Paper of 1939, Jewish immigration was to be halted after the quota of 75,000 had been exhausted unless the Arabs agreed to its continuation. At the rate of immigration prevailing after the war, the quota would be completely exhausted in August 1945. The Jewish Agency called for the abrogation of the White Paper, unlimited Jewish immigration, and the establishment of a Jewish state in Palestine. British and American Zionists appealed to Prime Minister Churchill, to his successor Clement Attlee, and to President Truman to make possible the immediate entry into Palestine of 100,000 displaced Jews. In September of 1945 the British Cabinet announced that a maximum of 1,500 Jewish immigrants would be allowed to enter Palestine each month. The American Zionist Council immediately rejected the offer as inadequate and called on President Truman to assist in preventing what it termed a shameful injustice.

The views of Truman and Attlee on the Jewish refugee problem diverged widely. Faced by mounting troubles in the Arab East, particularly in Egypt, Attlee did not wish to add to these troubles by irritating the Palestinian Arabs further. He therefore maintained that the Jewish refugees in Europe should be resettled in Europe and elsewhere, rather than in Palestine. Truman, on the other hand, favored their immediate admission to Palestine and his apparent belief that this was the best solution seemed to be confirmed by the report of Earl G. Harrison, who, at Truman's request, had gone to Europe in June 1945 to investigate the condition of displaced persons. Mr. Harrison had reported that Palestine was defi-

37

nitely the first choice of the Jewish displaced persons as a place of resettlement.[1] Mr. Truman sent a copy of the Harrison report to Mr. Attlee on August 31, 1945. On October 19 Attlee proposed the creation of a joint Anglo-American Committee to explore the problem of resettlement of Jewish refugees in Palestine and elsewhere and to prepare a permanent solution for the Palestine problem for submission to the U.N. Truman agreed to U.S. participation in the Committee, provided that it produce speedy results and that it focus on Palestine as the potential settlement area and not on other areas.

In the meantime, the number of Jews in the displaced persons (DP) camps was growing. The American and British troops had discovered only about 30,000 Jews still alive in the death camps in Germany and Austria at the close of the war.* But almost immediately, Jews began to flow into the American zones of Germany and Austria from Eastern Europe, particularly from Poland, where anti-Semitism was active. The Anglo-American Committee found 98,000 Jews in the DP camps in the American zones and by April 1947, when the American military authorities closed the borders, there were more than 177,000 Jews in the American zones, comprising about one-fourth of the population of the camps.

The Anglo-American Committee submitted its report on April 22, 1946.[2] It did not recommend partition as a longterm solution of the Palestine problem; on the other hand, it recommended that Palestine be neither a Jewish state nor an Arab state. It recognized that Palestine was the object of a struggle between Jewish and Arab nationalisms and concluded that both the Arabs and the Jews were determined to erect a state in which one people dominated the other. The Committee believed the solution to be retention of the mandate pending the execution of a trusteeship agreement under the United Nations. It envisaged a long trusteeship so that Arab and Jew could be brought together and a form of government established under which neither would dominate the other. In addition, the form of government ultimately to be established should, under international guarantees, fully protect the interests of Christendom, Islam, and Judaism in the Holy Land.

*Approximately six million Jews were killed by the Nazis in territories that came under their control during World War II. See *American Jewish Year Book, 1947-1948*, p. 737.

The Anglo-American Committee also recommended that in the meantime the land transfer regulations of 1940 be revoked and that 100,000 immigration certificates be issued immediately to Jews who were victims of Nazi persecution. The Committee rejected the view that there should be no further Jewish immigration into Palestine without Arab acquiescence, but it refused to recommend an annual immigration quota after the immediate admission of 100,000, leaving the quota to be decided by the government of Palestine. It was the opinion of the Committee that although most of the Jewish DP's wished to go to Palestine, the country could not absorb them all and that the U.S. and U.K. Governments, in association with other countries, should attempt to find new homes for them.

President Truman welcomed the portion of the report calling for immediate admission of 100,000 Jewish refugees. The U.S. offered to transport them to Palestine and to help defray the costs of their resettlement. Prime Minister Attlee demurred on the question of the issuance of the 100,000 certificates, saying the report must be considered in its entirety. A joint Anglo-American technical committee met on July 10, 1946, to work out the details of the Anglo-American Committee's proposals. On July 25, 1946, the technical committee put forth the Morrison-Grady plan, named after Herbert Morrison and Henry Grady, the chief British and American experts.[3] The plan called for the creation in Palestine of a cantonal state, composed of an autonomous Jewish province, an autonomous Arab province, and two areas under direct control of the central government. The Jewish province would include the Jordan valley from Beit Shean northward, the coastal plain between Acre and Wadi Rubin, and a corridor connecting the two at Affula. The Arab province would include the rest of the country except for the two areas under control of the central government: the Negev south of Beersheba and the Dead Sea, and the Jerusalem enclave. The Jerusalem enclave would not have a corridor to the sea but would be confined to Jerusalem and Bethlehem.

According to the Morrison-Grady plan, the Arab province, the Jewish province, and the Jerusalem district would elect their own legislative bodies, but the chief ministers and cabinets of the two provinces would be appointed by the British High Commissioner, who would be head of the central government. All legislation would require the assent of the High Commissioner, and all matters related to defense, foreign relations, and customs and excise would be reserved to the central government. The executive and legislative powers of the central government would be exercised initially by the High Commissioner, assisted by a nominated executive council. As for immigration, the plan called for the immediate admission of 100,000 Jewish refugees, as soon as the Arabs approved the plan. Further immigration would be based on the recommendation of each province and its economic capacity to absorb immigrants, but the final say would rest with the central government.

The British Cabinet immediately approved the Morrison-Grady plan, but the Arabs rejected any solution that did not provide for an Arab Palestine. The Jewish Agency also rejected it, since it was evident that the Arabs would not accept it and that not only would the 100,000 not be admitted to Palestine but future immigration would continue to be heavily restricted. The executive of the Jewish Agency, meeting in Paris in early August, decided to counter with its own plan. It was willing to abandon its demands for the whole of Palestine, provided a large enough Jewish state was created in a partitioned Palestine. Under the Jewish Agency's proposals, the area alloted to the Jewish state would include the Jordan valley north of Beit Shean, the Galilee, the coastal plain, and the Negev. The rest of the country, comprising the hill districts of east and central Palestine and a corridor to the sea at Jaffa would go to the Arabs.[4] Interestingly enough, the Jewish Agency was willing to let Jerusalem be part of the Arab state. The British Government refused to consider the Jewish Agency's plan and issued invitations on August 15 to the Jewish Agency executive and the Arab Higher Committee to attend a conference in London to discuss the Morrison-Grady plan. As it turned out, neither chose to attend.

In the meantime, President Truman had decided that the Morrison-Grady plan was unworkable, and he sent a message to Prime Minister Attlee on August 12 informing him that the United States would not support it. At the same time, the United States was going into a Congressional election campaign. Critics were charging that the Administration was not being vigorous enough on the Palestine issue. Mr. Truman got word that New York's Governor Dewey, a candidate for ree-lection, was about to make a statement favoring the Zionist position, and he decided to anticipate him.[5] In his Yom Kip-pur message on October 4, 1946, Truman endorsed the Jewish Agency's plan and reiterated his stand in favor of the immedi-ate admission of 100,000 Jews to Palestine.[6]

The UNSCOP Plan

World War II had been a heavy drain on British resources and by the spring of 1947 Great Britain was already being forced to cut back on its overseas commitments, notably in Greece and India. Meanwhile, the situation in Palestine con-tinued to deteriorate, with terrorism seriously threatening the public order. Attlee now decided that the Palestine problem was unsolvable and on April 2, 1947, the U.K. requested that the Palestine question be placed on the agenda of the U.N. General Assembly at the next regular session. It also requested that a special session of the Assembly be convened at once to set up a special committee to prepare for the con-sideration of the question at the regular session. The special session of the General Assembly convened on April 28, 1947. The British delegate, Sir Alexander Cadogan, made clear to the Assembly that while the U.K. would accept the Assem-bly's recommendation on the Palestine question, the U.K. was not prepared to accept responsibility for carrying it out with a British administration and British forces unless the solution was acceptable to both the Arabs and the Jews.[7] Although the Arabs opposed it, the General Assembly on May 15 set up an eleven-member committee, designated the United Nations Special Committee on Palestine (UNSCOP) and composed of delegates from Australia, Canada, Czechoslovakia, Guatemala, India, Iran, the Netherlands, Peru, Sweden, Uruguay, and Yugoslavia.[8]

The UNSCOP conducted hearings, both public and private, from June 17 through July 23, 1947. The Arab Higher Committee refused to cooperate with the Commission and the Arab case was presented by representatives of various Arab governments. Both the Arabs and the representatives of the Jewish Agency recited familiar arguments. The Arabs claimed that the terms of the mandate were illegal and invalid.

41

They said that Palestine was an Arab country and they demanded that the mandate be terminated and that Palestine be transformed into an independent unitary state. The representatives of the Jewish Agency called for the establishment of a Jewish state in Palestine and Jewish immigration into Palestine, both before and after the creation of the Jewish state, subject only to the limitations imposed by the economic absorptive capacity of that state. The Jewish Agency representatives frankly recognized the difficulty in creating a Jewish state in all of Palestine in which Jews would be only a minority or in a part of Palestine in which they would at first have only a slight preponderance. Heavy stress was therefore placed on the right of Jewish immigration for political as well as humanitarian reasons.

The UNSCOP also heard the Anglican Bishop in Jerusalem, the Moderator of the Church of Scotland in Palestine, and the representative of the Custos of the Holy Land.* The representative of the Custos was concerned about the fate of the Holy Places in the event a non-Christian government, either Arab or Jewish, should emerge in Palestine. It was clear from the representative's testimony that the concern of the Custos was not primarily that the government itself might encroach upon the Holy Places but that the government might side with a Christian group (Orthodox or Armenian) having a rival claim in a particular Holy Place. The representative of the Custos refrained from endorsing an international regime for Jerusalem. He said that while such a proposal might solve the problem for Jerusalem, it would not solve the problem of Holy Places in other areas of Palestine. He seemed to prefer some arrangement whereby diplomatic action might be brought into play if rights in the Holy Places were threatened and he kept referring to the role of protector played by France during the Ottoman period. The Anglican Bishop and the Scottish moderator showed more concern for the Christian minority than for the Holy Places. They felt that some arrangement should be made in the political orga-

*United Nations, A/364/Add. 2, pp. 135-138; and A/364/Add. 3, pp. 13-19. The Custos is the head of the Franciscan Fraternity of the Custodia di Terra Santa, which cares for those Holy Places in which the Latins have rights.

nization of the country whereby the Christians would have some form of recourse if they felt their rights were threatened.

On August 31, the Special Committee submitted two plans to the General Assembly.[9] The majority plan, supported by Canada, Czechoslovakia, Guatemala, the Netherlands, Peru, Sweden, and Uruguay, called for the division of Palestine into an Arab state, a Jewish state, and an international zone. The Jewish state would include Eastern Galilee, the upper Jordan Valley, the coastal plain between Acre and Ashdod, and the Negev. Except for the international zone, the rest of the country would go the Arab state. The international zone would be composed of Jerusalem, Bethlehem, and their rural suburbs. The Jewish state, the Arab state, and the international zone would be members of an economic union. During a two-year transition period beginning on September 1, 1947, the U.K. would carry on the administration of Palestine under U.N. auspices. At the end of the transition period, the Arab and the Jewish states would become independent, while the international zone would be placed under the international trusteeship system by means of a trusteeship agreement, which would designate the U.N. as the administering authority.

The minority plan, supported by the delegates of India, Iran, and Yugoslavia, provided for development of the mandate during a three-year transitional period into an independent federal state composed of a Jewish province and an Arab province, with Jerusalem as the federal capital.[10] A peculiar feature of the minority plan called for the partition of Jerusalem into two separate municipalities. One would include the Walled City and the Arab sections of the modern city outside the walls. The other municipality would be composed of the predominantly Jewish sections of the city outside the walls. The Arab and Jewish municipalities of Jerusalem would jointly provide such common public services as sewage, garbage collection and disposal, fire protection, water supply, local transport, and telephone and telegraph service. Although Article 8 of the mandate instrument provided for the revival of capitulations upon the termination of the mandate, the UNSCOP thought this was an anachronism and neither plan provided for it. The minority plan envisaged the creation of a permanent international body to supervise and protect the Holy Places.

Ordinarily, the General Assembly would have referred the UNSCOP report to the First Committee (Political Committee), but that committee was going to be occupied with the Greek question. Therefore, the General Assembly on September 23, 1947, set up the Ad Hoc Committee on the Palestinian Question, composed, like the First Committee, of all the member states of the U.N.[11] The Committee began its work by hearing statements by the British representative, a representative of the Arab Higher Committee, and a representative of the Jewish Agency. The British representative said at once that the British position had not changed. The U.K. was ready to assume responsibility for giving effect to any plan to which both the Arabs and Jews had agreed, but it would not feel able to implement any plan on which there was not such agreement. Should the General Assembly recommend a plan on which there was no agreement, it would be necessary to provide for some alternative authority to implement it. Further, in order that there be no misunderstanding, he had been instructed to announce in all solemnity that in the absence of an agreed settlement, the U.K. planned an early withdrawal of British troops and British administration from Palestine.

The representative of the Arab Higher Committee told the Ad Hoc Committee that the Arabs rejected both the majority and minority plans. He called for the immediate establishment of an independent Arab state in the whole of Palestine.[12] The Jewish Agency representative rejected the minority plan. As for the majority plan, he announced that while it was really not satisfactory to the Jewish people, the Agency was prepared to recommend it, saying that this "heavy sacrifice . . . would be the Jewish contribution to the solution of a painful problem."[13] He urged, however, that modern Jerusalem outside the walls be included in the Jewish state. He also welcomed the U.K.'s decision for early withdrawal, recommending that the two-year transition period be reduced as much as possible and that an international authority be entrusted with the task of administering Palestine during the transition period.

On October 11, the U.S. representative, Herschel Johnson,

announced to the Ad Hoc Committee U.S. support of the majority plan, and Semyon Tsarapkin informed the Committee on October 13 that the U.S.S.R. also supported the majority plan. With the minority plan thus rejected by the Jews, the Arabs, the U.S., and the U.S.S.R., little attention was given to it in the Ad Hoc Committee. The result was the appointment on October 22 of two subcommittees, the first to submit to the full Ad Hoc Committee a detailed plan based on the majority report of UNSCOP and the second to submit a detailed plan based on Iraqi, Saudi, and Syrian proposals for the creation of a unitary Palestinian state. The two subcommittees made their reports to the Ad Hoc Committee on November 19, 1947.

The report submitted by Subcommittee I made only slight changes in the majority plan of UNSCOP.[14] The boundaries of the Arab and Jewish states were modified slightly to reduce the size of the Arab minority in the Jewish state. The Arab portions of Jaffa were excluded from the Jewish state and made an enclave belonging to the Arab state. In the Subcommittee recommendations, the mandate in Palestine should end no later than August 1, 1948, and the transition period between the end of the mandate and the independence of the two states in Palestine was reduced from two years to two months. Administration during the transition period was to be carried out by a U.N. commission composed of Guatemala, Iceland, Norway, Poland, and Uruguay, which in turn would transfer it to the Jewish and Arab states as the administrative organs of the new states were established.

Under Subcommittee I's recommendations, the international zone was to be placed under a special international regime in relation with the Trusteeship Council, rather than under an international trusteeship agreement as recommended by UNSCOP. Referred to as the City of Jerusalem, it was to be a *corpus separatum* and to have a statute detailed and approved by the Trusteeship Council. The governor would be appointed by and responsible to the Trusteeship Council. There would be a legislative council elected on the basis of universal and secret suffrage by adult residents irrespective of nationality. The legislative council would have the power of legislation and taxation, but the governor would have the power to veto any bills inconsistent with the statute of the city and he would also have the power to promulgate temporary ordinances in case the legislative council failed to adopt in time a bill deemed essential to the normal functioning of the administration. Freedom of entry and residence was guaranteed to the citizens and residents of the Arab and Jewish states, but immigration into and residence within the city for nationals of other states would be controlled by the governor under the directions of the Trusteeship Council. Citizens of the Arab and Jewish states resident in the city would also have the right to vote in their respective states as well as in Jerusalem. Arabic and Hebrew would be the official languages of the city. After ten years, the special regime for the City of Jerusalem would be subject to revision and the residents would be free to express by means of a referendum their wishes as to the continuation or modification of the regime of the city.

Subcommittee II recommended to the Ad Hoc Committee that Palestine be constituted as a unitary state within one year, with adequate representation in the legislative for all important sections of the citizenry in proportion to their numerical strength.[15] According to Subcommittee II, there were 608,230 Jews in Palestine out of a total population of 1,972,560, but the Subcommittee left it to a Palestinian constituent assembly to determine the length of time one had to be a continuous legal resident in order to be eligible for citizenship. The constitution would be required to contain guarantees for the sanctity of the Holy Places covering inviolability, maintenance, freedom of access, and freedom of worship in accordance with the status quo of 1852.

The Ad Hoc Committee rejected Subcommittee II's recommendation for a unitary state and adopted, with minor modifications, Subcommittee I's partition plan.[16] The Jewish Agency representative renewed the offer he had made in Subcommittee I to transfer to the Arab state a portion of the Negev along the Egyptian frontier, if this would help make partition more palatable.[17] The U.S. delegate proposed that the Ad Hoc Committee amend the partition plan in accordance with this offer and the amendment was accepted. The Ad Hoc Committee also accepted a Norwegian-Pakistani amendment which would leave to the General Assembly the decision on the composition of the U.N. commission for the transition period. As for the City of Jerusalem, the Committee accepted a Swedish amendment to make the regime permanent.[18] The statute would be subject to reexamination, rather than revision, after ten years and the inhabitants would be free to express by means of a referendum their wishes as to possible modifications, rather than its continuation or modification. When the Ad Hoc Committee voted on Subcommittee I's plan as amended, it was favored by twelve out of twenty Latin American states, the East European states (except Yugoslavia), the Scandinavian states, Australia, Canada, South Africa, the U.S., and the U.S.S.R. It was opposed by the Muslim states, Cuba, India, Lebanon, and Siam. Among the abstainers were Belgium, France, and the U.K.[19]

On November 25, 1947, the Ad Hoc Committee forwarded its report to the General Assembly, where it was approved on November 29 by a vote of 33 to 10, with 10 abstentions.[20] Seven of those who abstained in the voting in the Ad Hoc Committee, including Belgium and France, voted for the partition plan in the General Assembly. Again, the U.S.S.R. voted affirmatively.

Soviet support for the partition plan and the emergence of a Jewish state represented a shift in Soviet policy. Prior to 1947, the U.S.S.R. had regarded Palestine as a secondary issue, artificially created by the Jewish problem in capitalist society. There was of course no such problem in Russia's socialist society. Zionism was condemned as a form of nationalism and therefore contrary to the cosmopolitanism of communist ideology. However, Soviet policy in the Near East after World War II was to reduce and eventually exclude Western, particularly British, influence from the area and perhaps ultimately to establish the area within the Russian sphere of influence. Despite British difficulties in Egypt, the Arabs, especially King Abdallah, were regarded by the Soviets as essentially pro-British. The Jews, on the other hand, had become embittered against Britain because of its restrictive Palestine immigration policy, and Jewish groups in Palestine were engaged in 1947 in active hostilities against the British authorities. In these circumstances, the Soviets in 1947 probably viewed the Jews of Palestine as permanently or sufficiently alienated from the British to serve as a vehicle for forwarding the Soviet objective of expelling the British from the area.*

---

*As a matter of fact, Israeli Colonel Yigael Yadin on February 14, 1949, urged that Israel and Egypt join in crushing British influence in the Near East. *The New York Times*, February 15, 1949.

47

The Draft Statute for Jerusalem

With the approval of the partition plan by the General Assembly, the scene of activity on the Jerusalem question now shifted to the Trusteeship Council. U.N. Secretary General Trygve Lie forwarded a copy of the General Assembly resolution to the Council on December 1, 1947, and called attention to the Council's responsibility for elaborating a statute for the City of Jerusalem. The following day, the Trusteeship Council appointed a Working Committee, composed of Australia, China, France, Mexico, the U.K., and the U.S., to draft a statute for Jerusalem. The Working Committee elected Benjamin Gerig of the U.S. as its Chairman, Sir Alan Burns of the U.K. as its Vice-Chairman, and Henri Laurentie of France as its Reporter.

The major problems faced by both the Working Committee and the full Trusteeship Council were those connected with the legislative council. The French probably saw the creation of an international regime in Jerusalem as an opportunity to regain a large measure of the influence lost in Jerusalem during the mandate and therefore sought to gain for the Christians as much influence as possible. Although the Christian population constituted less than 20 per cent of the population of the *corpus separatum*,[21] the French delegate suggested a legislative council composed of thirty members—ten Jewish, ten Muslim, and ten Christian members.[22]

Other members of the Working Committee felt that the legislative council should be divided on an ethnic, rather than a religious, basis. They therefore proposed a council of forty members, with eighteen seats each reserved for the Jewish and Arab communities and four seats reserved for those who were neither Jews nor Arabs. The U.S. favored a plan under which each of the three groups would nominate a number of candidates in excess of the number to be elected, and from each list the voter would vote for not more than the number of seats allotted to each group. Thus, all voters would participate in the election of all members. The Jews would help determine which Arabs would represent the Arabs and the Arabs would help determine which Jews would occupy the seats reserved for Jews. It was hoped that parties would therefore be formed cutting across electoral college lines. The other members felt that it would be better if three electoral groups were elected separately, since Arab women might not vote and the Jews would therefore have a disproportionate say in the election of members from the other two lists. In view of the lack of agreement on the legislative council, the Working Committee included all three alternatives in its draft statute and left it to the full Trusteeship Council to determine which alternative it preferred. The Working Committee approved its draft on January 23, 1948, published it on January 26, and submitted it to the full Trusteeship Council on February 16, 1948.[23]

When the draft statute was taken up by the full Trusteeship Council[24] on February 18, 1948, the Iraqi delegate reiterated at once the Arab position that Jerusalem was an integral part of Palestine, the partition plan was illegal, and any statute for a separate Jerusalem would be illegal.[25] Mr. Gerig replied that the General Assembly, rather than the Trusteeship Council, was the place to debate the general Palestine question, and that in preparing a draft statute for the City of Jerusalem the Trusteeship Council was simply carrying out the duties laid upon it by the General Assembly's resolution of November 29, 1947. Iraq withdrew from the discussion and the Trusteeship Council turned to consideration of the draft statute.

Since the draft statute had already been published, the Jewish Agency had already addressed a communication, dated February 2, to the Trusteeship Council, giving its observations on the draft, particularly Article 20 concerning the composition of the legislative council and the method of its election.[26] Two representatives of the Jewish Agency, Mordechai Eliash and Moshe Sharett (then Shertok),* restated these views before the Council on February 25.[27] They referred to the General Assembly's resolution of November 29, Part III, Section C, paragraph 5, providing for a legislative council elected on the basis of proportional representation. They interpreted the phrase "proportional representation" to mean political parties, rather than religious or ethnic groups. They pointed out that in the Municipality of Jerusalem under the mandate, Jews constituted a large majority of the population

---

*Mr. Sharett, like many Israelis, Hebraicized his name after the establishment of the state of Israel. Dov Joseph was formerly Bernard Joseph; Golda Meir was Goldie Myerson; Abba Eban (pronounced éh-ven) was Aubrey Eban (ee-báhn); etc. For the sake of convenience, only the Hebraicized name is used in this study for each individual.

and that even in the enlarged areas under the *corpus separatum*, half of the population was Jewish.† In these circumstances, if the seats in the legislative council were divided on a fixed ratio and according to a religious or ethnic basis, the Jews would want at least half the seats. The French representative told the Jewish Agency representatives that he favored a legislative council composed of equal numbers of Muslims, Christians, and Jews. He recognized that this would give the Christians undue influence in proportion to their numbers at first, but he expected an influx of Western Christians once the international city was established, thus altering the present religious ratio. The Jewish Agency representative thought that Christian interests would be adequately protected through a simple system of proportional representation and that there was no need to establish a fixed ratio on the legislative council.

Eliash and Sharett also took issue wth the provision of the draft statute which restricted the membership of the legislative council to citizens of Jerusalem. Since the partition plan and the draft statute would make all adult residents eligible to vote, they felt that membership in the legislative council should not be restricted to citizens. In their view, the General Assembly had not intended to create a new nationality, since Jerusalem was to be international, but had meant only to provide a citizenship for stateless persons in Jerusalem. Further, they expected the vast majority of the population to opt for citizenship in either the Jewish or the Arab states, so that only a few would be citizens of Jerusalem and hence eligible under the draft statute to sit in the legislative council. They therefore favored making all residents of the City eligible for election to the legislative council.

The Belgian representative agreed with the Jewish Agency representatives that residence rather than citizenship should be the basis of eligibility for the legislative council.[28] He also

†Total population of the *corpus separatum* just prior to the Palestine War was approximately 205,000, of which 100,000 were Jews, 65,000 were Muslims, and 40,000 were Christians. In Jerusalem itself, the Mandatory Government estimated the population to be 164,440, broken down as follows: 99,320 Jews, 33,680 Muslims, 31,320 Christians, and 110 others. See United Nations, A/1286, pp. 13 and 17; and Palestine, *Supplement to Survey of Palestine; Notes Compiled for the Information of the United Nations Special Committee on Palestine*, p. 13.

shared the view that the partition plan called for proportional representation based on parties, rather than on a religious or ethnic basis. He believed that a fixed division based on a religious or ethnic basis would not be democratic and would hinder the development of normal democratic life. Even if, at first, voting was along religious lines, the legislative council would automatically be divided on religious lines, without having it artificially fixed by a provision of the statute. The other members of the Trusteeship Council, however, were concerned that Arab women would not vote and hence the Arabs would be outvoted. They were also fearful that the Arabs might not cooperate in the Jerusalem plan unless their interests were protected beforehand in the statute.

In the end, the Council accepted a compromise proposed by Mr. Gerig, providing for a 40-member legislative council, with 18 members elected quadrennially by the Jews, 18 members by the Arabs, and one or two members elected by those who are neither Jews nor Arabs.[29] The remaining members would be members-at-large, elected by the entire electorate from a panel of six residents nominated by the governor from among those not registered in either the Arab or the Jewish group. Provision was also made for separate elections for the Christians and Muslims in proportion to their number for the 18 Arab seats if the governor felt that either group wanted separate elections. Residents and citizens 25 years of age or over were made eligible for the council. In order to prevent either the Jewish or the Arab states from flooding the international city with temporary residents to take part in elections or the referendum at the end of the first ten years, it was decided that those who were living in the *corpus separatum* on November 29, 1947, would be residents. Those who came after that date or who would come in the future would have to live in Jerusalem three years before they were eligible to become residents. Provision was also made for revision of the article on the composition and method of election of the legislative council prior to expiration of the initial ten-year period if circumstances warranted.

The Trusteeship Council completed its work on the draft statute on March 9 and adopted a resolution on March 10 to the effect that it was then in satisfactory condition but that the question of its formal approval and the appointment of the governor of Jerusalem should be deferred until a subsequent meeting to be held not later than one week before April 29.[30]

Jerusalem in Limbo

In the meantime, news of the General Assembly's resolution of November 29, 1947, recommending partition had produced an explosive situation in Palestine and the country had fallen into disorder. The British Colonial Secretary announced to Parliament in mid-December that the Palestine mandate would be terminated on May 15, 1948. The U.N. Commission to administer Palestine during the transition period had been appointed; but the British Government, pointing out that the Arabs had rejected the partition plan and the internationalization of Jerusalem, refused to transfer any authority to the U.N. Commission prior to May 15 and advised the members of the Commission not to go to Palestine before May 1.

On February 16, the U.N. Commission for Palestine reported to the Security Council that it would be unable to discharge its responsibilities at the close of the mandate without armed assistance.[31] On the other hand, the U.S. had just demobilized and U.S. Secretary of Defense James Forrestal warned President Truman that the U.S. could not afford to commit more than a token force to Palestine without partial remobilization. At the same time, he pointed out that implementation of the U.N. resolutions with the aid of U.S. troops would alienate the Arabs and might cause them to deny the U.S. access to oil.[32] The U.K. had already expressed its unwillingness to use its troops for this purpose. Having just been forced out of Syria and Lebanon, French troops in Palestine would have been an unwelcome prospect for the U.K. and the U.S. In view of the U.S.S.R.'s recent moves in the Near East, Soviet troops would likewise have been unwelcome.

It was against this background that Warren Austin, the U.S. delegate to the U.N., proposed in the Security Council on March 19, 1948, that the Council call on the Secretary General to convoke a special session of the General Assembly to consider placing the whole of Palestine under a temporary trusteeship in order to afford a further opportunity to reach an agreement between the interested parties and thereby bring about a peaceful settlement.* The Jewish Agency described Austin's proposal as a shocking reversal of the U.S. position which would incalculably hurt the prestige of the United Nations. U.N. Secretary General Trygve Lie was so upset at the supposed damage done to U.N. prestige by the "American reversal," that he threatened to resign and suggested to Austin that he too resign. Austin refused to resign and advised Lie not to either.[33] The Soviet delegate, Mr. Gromyko, accused the United States of attempting to bury the partition plan and seeking under the guise of a temporary trusteeship to convert Palestine into an Anglo-American military base. He called for immediate steps to implement partition. On April 1, 1948, the Security Council passed a resolution which, although it omitted any reference to a temporary trusteeship, nevertheless called on the Secretary General to convoke a special session of the General Assembly "to consider further the question of the future government of Palestine."[34]

The special session of the General Assembly convened on April 16, and the Palestine question was referred on April 19 to the First Committee, which considered it under two aspects: the future government of Palestine, and measures to protect Jerusalem. The question of the protection of Jerusalem was the more complicated one. The Jewish areas of the city had been under virtual siege since February 1948, and during the opening meeting of the special session, the Swedish representative called on the First Committee to treat the problem of maintaining order in Jerusalem and protecting the

*United Nations, Security Council, *Official Records; Third Year*, No. 46, 271st meeting. Truman gives the impression in his *Memoirs* that he did not know that Austin was going to make this proposal, and he says that anybody in the State Department should have known that it was at odds with his policy on Palestine. See Truman, *Memoirs*, Vol. II, p. 163. However, there is convincing evidence that Truman did know about the proposal. In fact, Secretary of State George Marshall informed Austin on March 8 that the President had approved a State Department draft of the statement. Truman was apparently embarrassed by the timing, not realizing when he assured Chaim Weizmann on March 18 of continued U.S. support for the partition plan that Austin was going to present the trusteeship proposal the following day. He complained to the State Department on March 20 about not being informed in advance when Austin was to speak. See John Goodall Snetsinger, "Truman and the Creation of Israel," unpublished doctoral dissertation, Stanford University, October 1969, pp. 103-6.

Holy Places as urgent, without prejudice to the larger issue. Since the Trusteeship Council was already familiar with the problem, having prepared a draft statute, the First Committee recommended and the General Assembly adopted a resolution referring the question to the Trusteeship Council.[35]

Two proposals now came before the Trusteeship Council, the first being the U.S. proposal for placing Jerusalem under temporary trusteeship with the provision for the maintenance of law and order. France proposed the immediate dispatch to Jerusalem of a United Nations official with powers to recruit, organize, and maintain an international force of 1,000 police. The Arab Higher Committee informed the Council that the Arabs opposed both proposals. The Australian representative suggested that the draft statute for Jerusalem be approved and that such portions of it as were applicable in the circumstances be brought into force. The Arab Higher Committee rejected this also. Finally, on May 3, the U.K. representative told the Council that provision might be made for carrying on the minimum necessary administrative services in Jerusalem after May 15 through the appointment under Palestinian legislation of a neutral person, acceptable to both Jews and Arabs, as Special Municipal Commissioner to carry out the functions previously performed by the Municipal Commission. The appointment could be made by the British High Commissioner in Palestine prior to May 15. The Trusteeship Council recommended this last course of action to the General Assembly on May 5. In doing so, the Trusteeship recognized that the Special Municipal Commissioner would not have the function of maintaining order, but it noted that a cease-fire in Jerusalem had been negotiated.[36]

On May 6, the General Assembly adopted the Trusteeship Council's report and also asked that the First Committee give continuing urgent attention to the question of further measures for the protection of Jerusalem and its inhabitants.[37] At the suggestion of the U.S., the First Committee set up a subcommittee on May 11 to consider the question. The U.K. informed the subcommittee that the Municipal Government of Jerusalem had issued an order dated that same day by which a Special Municipal Commissioner, to be nominated by the British High Commissioner or by the U.N., might take any action and give any directions which in his discretion he deemed appropriate for the administration of Jerusalem. Having failed to obtain approval from the Trusteeship Council of the U.S. proposal to place Jerusalem under temporary trusteeship, the U.S., with the cooperation of France, proposed in the First Committee's subcommittee on Jerusalem that the city be placed under a temporary international regime based upon Chapter XII of the U.N. Charter. The subcommittee accepted the joint American-French proposal and reported it to the full First Committee on May 13. Under the subcommittee's recommendation, the U.N. would be designated as the administering authority for Jerusalem, with full powers of administration, legislation, and jurisdiction.[38] These powers would be exercised through the Government of Jerusalem, consisting of a U.N. Commissioner and such officers as might be appointed by him or by the U.N. The Special Municipal Commissioner would continue his functions under the authority of the U.N. Commissioner. The temporary arrangement would terminate on December 31, 1949, unless otherwise determined by the General Assembly.

In the meantime, a subcommittee in the First Committee had been considering the question of the future government of Palestine. This subcommittee, like the subcommittee on Jerusalem, also completed its work and made its report to the First Committee in the late afternoon of May 13.[39] Members of the First Committee noted that the General Assembly would have to complete its work by 6:00 P.M. Eastern Daylight Time on May 14 because this corresponded to midnight May 14-15 Palestine time, when the mandate would terminate. The Chairman of the First Committee therefore wanted to take up the subcommittees' reports immediately and to consider the report on Jerusalem first, since it was presented first. But the representatives of Poland, the U.S.S.R., the Ukraine, and Uruguay objected on the grounds they had not had time to study either subcommittee's report. The First Committee therefore held a night meeting on May 13; but priority was given to the report of the subcommittee on the future of Palestine. The report on Jerusalem was not considered until May 14.

When the report on Jerusalem was taken up, the U.K. representative informed the First Committee that Mr. Harold

Evans, a distinguished Quaker from Philadelphia, had been appointed, with the agreement of both the Jews and the Arabs, as the Special Municipal Commissioner under the Jerusalem Municipal Government Order of May 11.[40] The U.S. and French representatives said that desirable as this appointment was, it did not constitute adequate assurance for the protection of Jerusalem, particularly in view of the uncertain legal status of the Commissioner's authority following the expiration of the mandate, and even more important, the precarious legal situation that might arise with respect to the appointment of a successor to Mr. Evans should he be obliged for some reason to give up the post. It was for this reason that they had proposed a temporary international regime for the city. The Jewish Agency representative informed the Committee that the proclamation of the Jewish state had already been signed in Tel Aviv at 10 o'clock Eastern Daylight Time that morning (4 P.M. Palestine time), explaining that the hour of the signing had been advanced out of respect for the Sabbath, which would begin at sundown.* The representative of Guatemala reiterated that the proposal for the special regime for Jerusalem would have to be adopted before the expiration of the mandate,—by 6 P.M. Eastern Daylight Time—since otherwise there would exist no possibility in international law of making any special arrangement for Jerusalem. The First Committee then adopted a motion by the representative of the U.S. that the First Committee forward the subcommittee's report to the General Assembly without a recommendation.

The General Assembly met immediately in plenary session to consider the First Committee's report.[41] The representative of the U.S. noted that the General Assembly had only one hour before the termination of the mandate and proposed that the First Committee's report on Jerusalem be considered before the report on the future government of Palestine. The motion carried and discussion on Jerusalem began with the proposal for temporary administration being supported by France and the U.S. and opposed by Egypt, Iraq, Syria, Afghanistan, Yemen, Poland, and the Ukraine. A vote was called for; but before the vote could proceed, the representative of Iraq took the floor to say that the time was one minute past 6 P.M. and that therefore "the whole game" was up. The

*Strict observance of the Jewish Sabbath precludes writing.

vote was taken anyway. The proposal was defeated and Jerusalem was left as a *corpus separatum* under the terms of the General Assembly's resolution of November 29, 1947. However, it had no statute and no governor. It had only a Special Municipal Commissioner.

The General Assembly then moved on to a discussion of the First Committee's report on the future government of Palestine. It was during the debate on this question that the U.S. delegate, Mr. Jessup, announced that President Truman had recognized the state of Israel. The First Committee had rejected the U.S. proposal for a temporary trusteeship, and the Committee's report proposed a resolution empowering a U.N. mediator in Palestine to promote a peaceful solution to the situation. The resolution was adopted by the General Assembly during the evening of May 14.[42] By the same resolution the Palestine Commission previously appointed under the General Assembly's 1947 partition resolution was relieved of further responsibility. A committee of the Assembly, composed of China, France, the U.S.S.R., the U.K., and the U.S. met on May 20, 1948, and appointed Count Folke Bernadotte, President of the Swedish Red Cross, as U.N. mediator in Palestine.

Chapter 4

The Partition of Jerusalem

The Special Municipal Commissioner

On May 15, 1948, the armies of Egypt, Jordan,[1] Syria, Iraq, and Lebanon crossed the frontiers of Palestine and engaged the forces of Israel in combat. The Egyptian Government informed the Security Council by a telegram dated May 15 that the Egyptian forces had intervened in Palestine "to establish security and order in place of chaos and disorder which prevailed and which rendered the country at the mercy of the Zionist terrorist gangs who persisted in attacking peaceful Arab inhabitants."[2] Despite the efforts of the U.N., Jerusalem was not spared the trials of war. In fact, serious fighting had taken place in the city in the spring, as both the Arabs and the Jews jockeyed for the best possible position before the end of the mandate. A truce had been arranged for the Walled City on May 2 and was extended to the whole city a week later. However, the truce was shaky at best and collapsed on May 15.

In view of the late date on which Harold Evans was appointed Special Municipal Commissioner for Jerusalem, Dr. Pablo Azcárate y Florez, already in place as an advance member of the U.N. Palestine Commission, was appointed temporary Special Municipal Commissioner until Evans could assume his duties. Evans also explained to Azcárate that he had accepted the appointment on condition that he not be required to assume his functions until peace was restored, since, as a Quaker, he was not certain he could accept the protection of a military escort.[3] Evans therefore went to Cairo to await the restoration of peace.

Azcárate bravely and vigorously assumed the duties of the Municipal Commissioner, but in the circumstances, his mission proved to be an impossible one. He had no military forces at his disposal with which to restore or even maintain order.

The Jewish part of the city had been organized as a municipality before the departure of the British with Dr. Daniel Auster as Mayor, and this part of the city offered to cooperate with Azcárate. But in the Arab sections there was no such organization, and when the Arab Legion arrived a few days later, the Commandant, Abdallah al-Tall, refused to cooperate. Colonel Tall explained that war prevailed and that there could therefore be no other authority than the military. Azcárate went to Amman where he appealed to King Abdallah for cooperation, but the king made it clear that there was no question of accepting or recognizing any kind of international authority in Jerusalem. As far as he was concerned, Jerusalem belonged to him. Azcárate went to Cairo on June 4 and reported to Evans. After a short visit to Jerusalem with the U.N. mediator, Count Bernadotte, Evans resigned as Special Municipal Commissioner and returned to the U.S. Azcárate remained in Cairo, where he was appointed by Bernadotte as his representative to Egypt and the Arab League. The post of Special Municipal Commissioner lapsed.

Bernadotte's Preliminary Proposals

The U.S.S.R. was indignant at the turn of events in Palestine. It accused the Arab governments of aggression and called on them to desist. This stand was taken repeatedly in *Pravda* and *Izvestia* from May 15 to May 25. King Abdallah was called a British stooge. The U.S. was accused of secretly collaborating with Britain against Israel, and the U.S.S.R. was described as the only true friend of Jewish national independence.

With the support of the U.N. Security Council, Count Bernadotte was able to arrange a truce which began on June 11 at 8 A.M. (Palestine time). On June 28 and 29, Bernadotte presented to the Arab League and to Israel brief papers setting forth his suggestions for a Palestine settlement.[4] The plan provided for the transformation of the original Palestine mandate—that is, Jordan and Palestine—into a union composed of two members, one Arab and one Jewish. The whole or major part of the Negev would be included in the territory of the Arab member while the whole or part of Western Galilee would be included in Jewish territory. The question of

59

immigration would be completely within the competence of the Arab and Jewish members of the union for the first two years. After that, either member could request the Council of the Union to review the immigration policy of the other and to render a ruling in terms of the common interests of the union.

As for Jerusalem, Bernadotte reasoned that since the city stood in the heart of what must be Arab territory in any partition of Palestine, to attempt to isolate it politically and otherwise from surrounding territory would present enormous difficulties.[5] In a conversation with French Foreign Minister Bidault in Paris on May 26, 1948, while enroute to take up his duties in Palestine, Bernadotte discussed the possibility of including Jerusalem in the Arab state. Bidault let the Count know in no uncertain terms that he opposed such a scheme.[6] Undaunted by the negative French reaction, Bernadotte suggested that Jerusalem be included in the Arab state.

Although Bernadotte termed his suggestions highly tentative, he presented them formally and simultaneously to both sides with a covering statement, noting:

> I should make perfectly clear my intentions as regards future procedure. If it develops that the suggestions herewith presented, or other suggestions subsequently presented, which may arise from reactions to those now put forth, provide a basis for discussion, I will carry on with the discussions as long as may prove necessary and fruitful. If, however, these or subsequent suggestions, if any should emerge, are rejected as a basis for discussion, which I earnestly hope will not occur, I shall promptly report the circumstances fully to the Security Council and shall feel free to submit such conclusions to the Security Council as I may consider appropriate.[7]

Reaction to the Preliminary Proposals

The majority of the Jewish population of Jerusalem were ready at the end of 1947 to implement the U.N. provision for the internationalization of Jerusalem.[8] Although they did not like it, many saw it as the price to be paid for U.N. approval of the partition plan and the establishment of a Jewish state. Besides, it might prove in the end to be only a temporary inconvenience and lead to the eventual inclusion of the whole city, instead of just part of it, within the Jewish state. They noted that, according to the General Assembly resolution, the Jerusalem regime was to be reexamined at the end of the first ten years and that the residents of Jerusalem were to be free "to express by means of referendum their wishes as to possible modifications of the regime of the city."[9] Since the Jewish population of the *corpus separatum* at the end of 1947 was only slightly less than half the total, the opening of the gates of immigration would soon produce a Jewish majority and a referendum would almost certainly result in a vote for inclusion within the Jewish state.[10] A committee of eight was appointed by the Jewish Agency and the Vaad Leumi (the national council of the Jewish community in Palestine) to work with the U.N. in setting up the international regime in Jerusalem.[11] Discussions were begun in December 1947 among the Jewish leaders as to where the government of the proposed Jewish state would establish itself.[12] David Ben-Gurion favored Kurnub in the Negev, while Golda Meir preferred Mount Carmel. Nathanya, Zichron Yaaqov, and Herzliya were also considered, but underlying these considerations was the conviction that only Jerusalem could be the capital of Israel. What was being considered was only a site for the seat of government. Finally, the Emergency Committee, set up by the Vaad Leumi and the Jewish Agency to prepare for the new state, decided in early February 1948 that the seat of government would be in Sarona, a suburb of Tel Aviv.[13]

By the end of June 1948 Jewish Jerusalem had survived a long siege and few took seriously now the talk about internationalization. To be sure, the ultraorthodox Jews regarded the restoration of Israel as the proper work of the Messiah and human activity to that end as impious, and they favored internationalization of Jerusalem as a way out of the dilemma created for them by the proclamation of the state in Tel Aviv. But, on the whole, most felt that in the fullness of time West Jerusalem would be included in Israel.* The Provisional Government of Israel was reluctant to take any

*The terms "West Jerusalem" and "East Jerusalem" are used in this study simply for convenience in designating the areas of the city under Israeli and Jordanian control, respectively, at the close of the Palestine War.

action, however, for fear that it would complicate its relations with the United Nations.[14]

Bernadotte's June proposals provoked a severe reaction both in West Jerusalem and in the Provisional Government in Tel Aviv. The proposals were rejected by the Provisional Government in the most categorical of terms. In a letter dated July 5, 1948, and addressed to the U.N. mediator, Israel's Foreign Minister Sharett said:

> The Provisional Government was deeply wounded by your suggestion concerning the future of the City of Jerusalem, which it regards as disastrous. The idea that the relegation of Jerusalem to Arab rule might form part of a peaceful settlement could be conceived only in utter disregard of history and of the fundamental facts of the problem. . . . The Provisional Government must make it clear that the Jewish people, the State of Israel, and the Jews of Jerusalem will never acquiesce in the imposition of Arab domination over Jerusalem, no matter what formal municipal autonomy and right of access to the Holy Places the Jews of Jerusalem might be allowed to enjoy. They will resist any such imposition with all the force at their command. The Provisional Government regrets to have to say that your startling suggestion regarding Jerusalem, by encouraging false Arab hopes and wounding Jewish feelings, is likely to achieve the reverse of the pacifying effect which you undoubtedly had in mind.[15]

The U.S.S.R. and the Ukraine supported Israel and denounced the Bernadotte proposals as an effort to truncate Israel by removing the Negev and to restore British control in the area through Jordan.[16]

In West Jerusalem, feeling began to mount during the first part of July 1948. Even the moderates were shocked by Bernadotte's proposal that the entire city be given to King Abdallah, and the extremists represented by the Revisionists urged outright annexation of Jerusalem by Israel. The issue was debated in the Municipal Council of West Jerusalem on July 15 and the Council decided to call on the Provisional Government of Israel to make West Jerusalem part of the state of Israel.[17] Partially responding to the Municipal Council's request, the Provisional Government issued two proclamations on August 2, 1948, one declaring that West Jerusalem was "Israel-occupied territory"[18] and the other appointing

Dov Joseph as Military Governor.[19] The first proclamation noted that the U.N. had failed to provide a legal framework for Jerusalem and that the action of the Provisional Government was designed to fill this gap for the portion under Jewish control. The proclamation was therefore made retroactive to 12:01 A.M., May 15.

Bernadotte's preliminary proposals not only brought him the cordial dislike of the Jewish inhabitants of Jerusalem but also resulted in a general suspicion among the Israelis of the actions and intentions of the U.N. officials in Palestine. Bernadotte was both vexed and astonished at the Jewish reaction, and at a private luncheon with Foreign Minister Moshe Sharett on August 10, 1948, he talked bluntly and openly to Sharett about the Israeli attitude to the U.N. group. Sharett admitted that Bernadotte and the U.N. group were regarded in a way as "enemies." However, the Count's plea for understanding was ineffective in allaying Sharett's suspicions. Although the Israelis had indicated to Bernadotte at the beginning of the first truce that they were ready to discuss demilitarization of Jerusalem, they became particularly wary of such proposals after his Jerusalem proposal. They therefore consistently rejected them, while the Arabs reversed their position and agreed to discuss them. These proposals, put forth in various forms from July 22 on, provided, among other things, for the control of food supplies and for a military force under the control of the U.N. Truce Commission.* Military Governor Dov Joseph feared that once West Jerusalem was demilitarized and brought under the effective control of the Truce Commission, it would be unable to resist the mediator's plan to put the whole city under King Abdallah of Jordan.

Bernadotte's June proposals for a Palestine settlement received no better treatment from the Arab League than they did at the hands of the Israelis. Since these proposals were considered to be favorable to King Abdallah and an advance toward his Greater Syria plan, they were opposed by Egypt, Syria, and Saudi Arabia. King Abdallah appealed personally to Kings Ibn Saud and Faruq but the Political Committee of the Arab League, meeting in Cairo, rejected the plan and countered with the suggestion that a unitary state be created

*The Truce Commission was composed of the Consuls of the U.S., France, and Belgium in Jerusalem.

in Palestine, with safeguards for the Jewish minority. On September 20, the Arab League announced the formation of an "Arab Government of All Palestine," with Gaza as its headquarters and Ahmad Hilmi, the Jordanian Military Governor of Jerusalem, as Prime Minister and Foreign Minister.[20]

King Abdallah refused to recognize the Gaza Government and appointed Abdallah al-Tall to replace Ahmad Hilmi as Military Governor of Arab-held Jerusalem. On October 1, the "Palestine National Assembly" met in Gaza and elected Hajj Amin al-Husayni, the Mufti of Jerusalem, as President of the Assembly, while in Amman on the same day some 5,000 notables, claiming to represent the Palestine Arabs, met to denounce the Gaza Government and to call on King Abdallah to take Palestine under his protection. On November 15, while Abdallah was visiting the Coptic convent in the Walled City, he was crowned by the Coptic bishop and proclaimed "King of Jerusalem." Then the Second Palestine Arab Congress, meeting in Jericho on December 1, proclaimed Abdallah King of Palestine, and asked the king to take immediate steps to unite Palestine and Jordan.[21] The Jordanian Parliament gave its approval on December 13 for such a union and Prime Minister Abu al-Huda said that the implementation of the union would be carried out according to constitutional and legal procedures.[22] Since Hajj Amin was a member of the Gaza Government, King Abdallah appointed Shaykh Husam al-Din Jarallah, a former official of the Palestine Government, as Mufti of Jerusalem.

In the meantime, on September 12, 1948, Israeli Military Governor Dov Joseph was informed that Count Bernadotte planned to move his headquarters from Rhodes to Jerusalem so as to be nearer to the center of affairs. His office would be in Government House, which had been the residence of the British High Commissioners and which the departing High Commissioner, with the approval of Dr. Azcárate on behalf of the U.N., had turned over to the International Committee of the Red Cross for use as a security zone for noncombatants. Dov Joseph informed the U.N. that Haifa would be a less dangerous place for Bernadotte. U.S. Ambassador McDonald, who had taken up his duties in Israel on August 12, had voiced the same sentiment to Bernadotte on September 9. Nevertheless, Bernadotte arrived in Jerusalem on the afternoon of Friday, September 17. He visited Government House that afternoon and as he was returning to the YMCA through the Qatamon quarter of West Jerusalem, he was shot by members of the Stern Gang dressed as Israeli soldiers. He was immediately taken to Hadassah Hospital, where at 5:15 P.M. he was pronounced dead on arrival.

The Mediator's Report

The day before his assassination, Count Bernadotte had prepared a progress report for submission to the U.N. General Assembly and he forwarded it under a covering letter recommending that the Palestine question be included in the agenda of the General Assembly then about to convene in Paris.[23] In his report, he concluded that it would not be possible to create a political union in Palestine between Israel and an Arab state, as he had proposed earlier. While he conceded that Israel's boundaries must be fixed either by formal agreement between the parties or failing that, by the U.N., he continued to recommend the same territorial changes he had recommended earlier—that is, the Negev should go to the Arab state and Western Galilee should be given to Israel. He also thought that although the disposition of Arab Palestine should be decided by the Arab states in consultation with the Palestinian inhabitants, there were good reasons to recommend that it be merged with Jordan. In contrast to his earlier proposals, he now proposed that Jerusalem, because of its religious and international significance, be accorded special and separate treatment. It should, he said, be placed under effective United Nations control, but there should be maximum feasible local autonomy for its Arab and Jewish communities. In such an arrangement, he thought full safeguards must be provided for the protection of the Holy Places and for free access to them.

Bernadotte's new proposals were published on September 20. British Prime Minister Ernest Bevin completely endorsed the Bernadotte plan. U.S. Secretary of State George Marshall immediately characterized it as sound and a generally fair basis for the settlement of the Palestine issue, and on September 23 he urged the U.N. General Assembly to accept it in its entirety as the best possible means of bringing peace to a troubled land. The American position was subsequently reversed because President Truman thought Bernadotte's proposal to take the Negev from Israel was contrary to personal assurances he had given to Chaim Weizmann and to the Democratic platform on which he was then running for re-election.[24] His immediate reaction was to make a public statement reaffirming the Israel plank of the platform, but in order not to embarrass Secretary of State Marshall, he deferred it.* However, late in October he was charged by his opponent, Governor Dewey, with having reneged on the Democratic platform. Consequently, President Truman reaffirmed his position on Israel in a speech in Madison Square Garden on October 28.[25]

Military Governor Dov Joseph was concerned about the possible effects of the Bernadotte report on the future of West Jerusalem, particularly in light of the assassination. A martyr's report might command more sympathy at the U.N. Although the Provisional Government of Israel considered West Jerusalem to be Israel-occupied territory, this did not mean that the Government had been committed to its inclusion within the state of Israel. Prevailing sentiment in Jerusalem was for inclusion, but a few members of the cabinet of the Provisional Government were still ready to agree to internationalization of Jerusalem as the price to be paid for international support for Israel. Joseph now wanted to have the situation clarified as soon as possible and he headed a delegation from Israeli-held Jerusalem which appeared before the Provisional Government in Tel Aviv on September 26 to plead for a formal commitment. Three days later, the Military Governor took back to Jerusalem the Provisional Government's decision to insist at all costs on the inclusion of West Jerusalem within Israel. Major General Aage Lunstrom, who upon the death of Bernadotte became the U.N. mediator's representative, was informed by Joseph of the Provisional Government's decision on October 18.

Prime Minister Ben-Gurion and Foreign Minister Sharett were also troubled by the Bernadotte plan, particularly the

*The plank on Israel in the Democratic platform read: "We approve the claims of the State of Israel to the boundaries set forth in the United Nations resolution of November 29 and consider that modification thereof should be made only if fully acceptable to the State of Israel." *The New York Times*, July 15, 1948.

provisions on the Negev. Further, they realized that the Bernadotte assassination had cost Israel a great deal of the world sympathy it had previously enjoyed. The U.K. backed the plan and President Truman had not yet reversed Secretary of State Marshall's endorsement of it. If it were adopted by the U.N. General Assembly, Israel might well become an even smaller state than was envisaged in the resolution of November 29, 1947. The Israeli Army Chiefs therefore pushed for a campaign to secure the Negev. Sharett was opposed to the resumption of hostilities. Ben-Gurion was reluctant but was eventually persuaded. Taking advantage of the disarray in the Arab camp over who should govern Palestine, the Israelis in October and December 1948 expelled the Egyptians from the Negev and pushed into the Sinai Peninsula. In a similar operation in the north, the Lebanese were driven from Galilee and the Israelis occupied a number of villages in southern Lebanon.

The Vatican was deeply concerned about the hostilities in Palestine. While not as active as Pius XI in trying to bring the Orthodox into communion with Rome, Pope Pius XII had probably seen an internationalized Jerusalem as provided for by the partition plan as an opportunity for the Vatican to establish in the East a center of strong influence.[26] The Vatican was fearful lest the temporary division of Jerusalem between Jordan and Israel as a result of the hostilities harden into a permanent arrangement. On October 24, 1948, Pope Pius issued the first of his two encyclicals on Palestine, *In Multiplicibus.*[27] In this document, he expressed great sorrow over the war in the Holy Land as well as his apprehensions for the fate of the Christian population and the safety of Christian shrines. In a key paragraph, the pontiff suggested that "it would be expedient, as a better guarantee for the safety of the sanctuaries under the present circumstances, to give an international character to Jerusalem and its vicinity."[28]

Fait Accompli

In the U.N. General Assembly, Bernadotte's report was referred to the First Committee, where it was considered from November 15 to December 4. The U.K. proposed in the First Committee a draft resolution endorsing Bernadotte's conclusions and providing for the creation of a conciliation commission to assist the parties in arriving at a settlement based on those conclusions. The U.S.S.R. opposed both the Bernadotte proposals and the U.K. draft resolution and stated its preference for withdrawal of all foreign (Arab) forces from Palestine and direct negotiations between the Arabs and Israelis along the lines of the U.N. resolution of November 29, 1947.[29] These latter proposals were rejected. By this time, Israel was in firm control of both Western Galilee and Eastern Galilee, and Syria now did an about-face and submitted a draft resolution on November 26 providing for a commission to prepare proposals for the establishment of a single Palestinian state on a cantonal or federal basis similar to the minority UNSCOP plan which the Arabs had rejected in 1947.[30] Egypt supported the Syrian draft resolution, but it was also rejected.[31]

On December 4, the First Committee recommended to the General Assembly a revised form of the U.K. draft resolution omitting any endorsement of Bernadotte's conclusions. The resolution, as amended and adopted by the General Assembly on December 11, 1948, established a conciliation commission to be composed of three states nominated by a committee consisting of the five permanent members of the Security Council (China, France, the U.S.S.R., the U.K., and the U.S.). One of the functions of the commission was to present to the next regular session of the General Assembly detailed proposals for a permanent international regime for the Jerusalem area. Taking account of the changed circumstances, the resolution specified that the proposals should provide for "the maximum local autonomy for distinctive groups consistent with the special international status of the Jerusalem area."[32]

By the time the Palestine Conciliation Commission arrived in Palestine, the Egyptians had asked for a truce and armistice talks were already under way with the assistance of the Acting Mediator, Ralph Bunche. An armistice agreement between Egypt and Israel was signed on February 24, 1949, followed by an Israeli-Lebanese armistice agreement on March 23, an Israeli-Jordanian armistice agreement on April 3, and an Israeli-Syrian armistice agreement on July 20.[33] In the meantime, national elections were held in Israel on January 25, 1949, to replace the Provisional Government; and on February 2, Israeli-held Jerusalem was officially declared by the new government to be no longer considered as occupied territory and military rule was abolished.[34] On March 16, 1949, an agreement was signed by Jordan and Israel on the armistice lines in Jerusalem,[35] and on the same day, Jordan replaced military rule in its section of the city with civil administration.[36] Not only was Palestine now partitioned, but Jerusalem was partitioned as well.

Chapter 5

The U.N. Failure

The Palestine Conciliation
Commission Plan

In establishing the Palestine Conciliation Commission, the General Assembly had instructed it to assist the parties in achieving "a final settlement of all differences outstanding between them."[1] The Commission, composed of representatives of France, Turkey, and the U.S., arrived in Palestine and set up its headquarters in Jerusalem on January 24, 1949, at Government House, which had been turned over to the U.N. by the International Committee of the Red Cross when it withdrew from the city on September 30, 1948. Mark Ethridge represented the United States, Claude de Boisanger represented France, and Hüseyin Yalcin represented Turkey.[2] Inasmuch as the armistice negotiations had already begun, the Commission thought it best for the Acting Mediator to continue with the task of bringing them to a successful conclusion. The armistice agreements being negotiated were regarded as provisional and the first step toward a final peace settlement. Once they were concluded, the Conciliation Commission would take over and carry the armistice forward to peace.

The armistice negotiations took longer than the Conciliation Commission had anticipated, and the members of the Commission felt that it was important to get started on their mission. Accordingly, the Commission decided to begin with the task of settling two problems not directly connected with the armistice negotiations: Jerusalem and the refugees. An exchange of views with the representatives of the Arab League governments took place in Beirut from March 21 to April 5.[3] The Arab governments showed themselves, in general, prepared to accept the principle of an international regime for the Jerusalem area, but they reserved the right to give their final opinion after they were acquainted with the text of the proposals which the Commission would make. Israeli Prime Minister Ben-Gurion told the Commission on April 7 in Tel Aviv that Israel "for historical, political, and religious reasons" could not accept the establishment of a *corpus separatum* for Jerusalem.[4] He said that when Israel was in a position to do so, it intended to request the United Nations General Assembly to revise the part of the resolution of December 11, 1948, that dealt with Jerusalem. On the other hand, Ben-Gurion said that Israel would accept without reservation an international regime for, or the international control of, the Holy Places.

Israel's position was restated by Mr. Eban in the Ad Hoc Political Committee on May 5, 1949.[5] He said that the Government of Israel supported the suggestion that guarantees should be given for the protection of the Holy Places not only in Jerusalem but throughout Palestine. Israel, he said, was prepared to offer the fullest safeguards and guarantees for the security of religious institutions in the exercise of their functions and, with that end in view, was willing to negotiate immediately with all religious authorities concerned.

Meanwhile, the Vatican continued to oppose any plan for making permanent the division of Jerusalem between Jordan and Israel, since under such an arrangement, there would be little prospect for concentrating a Christian population in Jerusalem in sufficient numbers to have much say in the conduct of the affairs of the city or to provide a base for promotion of Vatican interests in the Near East.[6] Proposals for functional internationalization of the shrines were also not very appealing. The introduction of the authority of the U.N. into the already complicated picture of the Holy Places might only serve to erode Latin rights, especially since it would be difficult to control the composition of the U.N. commission for the Holy Places. What would happen to Latin rights, for example, if the U.N. commissioner were a non-Catholic? Consequently, Pope Pius issued his second encyclical on Palestine, *Redemptoris Nostri*, on April 15 restating his support for full territorial internationalization.[7] He urged all the faithful to exert every effort to see that their governments supported this course of action.

Exchanges between Israel and the Vatican took place in the summer of 1949, when Monsignor Thomas J. McMahon, head of the Catholic Near East Welfare Association, visited Israel, ostensibly on refugee matters.[8] Although Monsignor McMahon discussed the whole range of problems between the Vatican and Israel, he was especially interested in the Jerusalem question. He explained that the Vatican had been friendly to the 1947 partition plan with the understanding that Israel would abide by the provision for the full internationalization of Jerusalem. His argument was that only full internationalization of Jerusalem and its adjacent territory would make possible the repatriation of the Christian population, without which the Christian shrines would become only lifeless museum pieces. Only internationalization would permit the growth of Jerusalem as a universal Christian religious, cultural, and educational center. No information is available on Monsignor McMahon's talks with Jordanian officials.

On September 1, 1949, the Palestine Conciliation Commission forwarded to the Secretary General for submission to the General Assembly a draft instrument for a permanent international regime for the Jerusalem area.[9] In compliance with the General Assembly's resolution of December 11, 1948, the Commission had sought to provide as much local autonomy as possible. According to the plan, the City of Jerusalem, as defined in the resolutions of November 29, 1947, and December 11, 1948, would be permanently demilitarized and divided into two zones, one Arab and one Jewish. These zones would correspond in general with the areas held by Jordan and Israel. Administration of municipal affairs in the Arab zone would be in the hands of Jordan and in the Jewish zone in the hands of Israel, except in matters reserved for a U.N. commission and the international organs provided for by the instrument. Conscious of the fact that the U.S.S.R.'s permanent membership on the Trusteeship Council would afford the Soviet Union an opportunity to introduce a considerable measure of Soviet influence in Jerusalem if the U.N. authority in Jerusalem were to be responsible to the Trusteeship Council as proposed in the 1947 partition plan, the Palestine Conciliation Commission stipulated in its draft instrument that the U.N. commissioner be appointed by and be responsible to the General Assembly, rather than to the Trusteeship Council. There would be a general council for the City, composed of fourteen appointed members: five each by

Jordan and Israel and two from each zone by the U.N. commissioner. The general council would in general have a planning and coordination function for the entire City and could make rules for matters involving both sections. It would also have such other functions and powers entrusted to it by Jordan and Israel. A system of international courts was prescribed by the plan to deal with questions involving the Holy Places and legal conflicts arising from the two zones. Protection of the Holy Places, both within Jerusalem and in Palestine outside the City of Jerusalem, would fall within the competence of the U.N. commissioner. The instrument would also ban immigration which "might alter the present demographic equilibrium of the area of Jerusalem."[10]

Rejection of the Palestine Conciliation Commission's Plan

By the time the Palestine Conciliation Commission submitted its plan, the world was beginning to split between those who favored territorial internationalization of Jerusalem and those who favored some type of functional internationalization of the Holy Places. The Conciliation Commission's plan, being neither fully territorial nor fully functional in its approach, provoked criticism from both sides and helped further polarize the situation. Within a week of its publication, the plan was opposed by both the Arabs and the Israelis. Israeli Foreign Minister Moshe Sharett called it anachronistic and described the restriction on immigration to Jerusalem as unenforceable and a menace to Jerusalem's economic future.[11] He said the idea that the population of Jerusalem could be deliberately and artificially frozen in total size or in racial composition was utterly fantastic. He reiterated Israel's position that internationalization should be functional, rather that territorial, and limited to the Holy Places. The Arab states reversed their stand of 1947 and now supported full territorial internationalization as provided in the November 29, 1947, resolution. But King Abdallah, in Spain on a visit when the report was released, was being hailed as protector of the Holy Places. This made a deep impression on him, and he opposed the Palestine Conciliation Commission's plan when he returned to Jordan. He said in Amman on October 8 that Jerusalem would be internationalized only over his dead body, and he rejected internationalization again in a speech in Bethlehem on October 13.[12] By the time the Ad Hoc Political Committee began discussion of the Conciliation Commission's plan on November 24, Jordan was deeply involved in secret negotiations with Israel for a settlement that would include division of Jerusalem between the two.[13] Abdallah was asking Israel to cede the Jerusalem-Bethlehem road and the former Arab quarters of West Jerusalem. Israel was offering to make these concessions in exchange for the Jewish quarter of the Walled City. A settlement seemed to be in sight and Jordan was now even more opposed to internationalization, either territorial or functional.[14]

In view of the Vatican's stand, Roman Catholic countries, with certain notable exceptions, favored full territorial internationalization. Protestants and Protestant countries generally favored functional internationalization. An exception here was the Archbishop of Canterbury, who, speaking personally and not on behalf of the Church of England, put forth his own plan on October 31, 1949. According to his plan, internationalization would be more thoroughly territorial than in the Conciliation Commission's plan, but the area to be internationalized would be confined to the Walled City and the shopping area immediately surrounding it.[15] He recommended that the new city outside the walls, except for those small portions included in the international enclave, be incorporated in the state of Israel. The international enclave would not be divided into Arab or Jewish zones of local administration, although he said that facilities should be given for the return of the Jews to the Jewish quarter so that the Walled City would once again contain its Muslim, Jewish, and Christian quarters.

Another notable exception was Australia, where the Labour Government, facing national elections in 1949, was particularly mindful that some 21 per cent of the Australian electorate was Roman Catholic.[16] Consequently, on the first day of the discussion of the Palestine Conciliation Commission's plan in the Ad Hoc Political Committee, the Australian representative introduced a draft resolution with two objectives: first, to reaffirm the territorial internationalization provisions of the 1947 partition plan, and second, to enlarge the Palestine Conciliation Commission from three to seven members and to charge it to prepare within one year a plan for Jerusalem which could more nearly meet the conditions set forth in the partition plan.[17] Belgium and most of the Latin American countries supported the draft resolution. The Soviet representative, Mr. Tsarapkin, supported the implementation of the resolution of November 29, 1947, and said that this called for full territorial internationalization of Jerusalem. He therefore offered several amendments to the Australian draft resolution, one of which would eliminate the provision for enlarging the Palestine Conciliation Commission and would ask it to prepare a new plan.[18] Instead, it would simply call on the Trusteeship Council to revise the obsolete portions of the draft statute for Jerusalem and to approve it. Another of the Soviet amendments would dissolve the Palestine Conciliation Commission.

Both Jordan* and Israel rejected the Australian draft resolution, and Israel introduced its own draft resolution authorizing the Secretary General to conclude with Israel an agreement guaranteeing protection of the Holy Places in Israeli-controlled Jerusalem and providing for the appointment by the Secretary General of a United Nations representative to reside in Jerusalem and observe the agreement's implementation.[19] In introducing the resolution, the Israeli representative explained that since Israel was willing to agree to functional internationalization, the settlement of the status of the Holy Places in the Israeli part of Jerusalem need not await a parallel settlement concerning those in Arab hands. As for territorial internationalization, Mr. Sharett noted that the vast majority of the Holy Places were within the Walled City, which covered only 6.5 per cent of the municipal territory of Jerusalem. He suggested that if the Arab inhabitants of the Walled City could be induced by the offer of better housing to settle outside the walls, then the Walled City could be converted into a site containing only Holy Places and religious foundations, consecrated to religious worship and pilgrimage by members of all faiths.[20]

*Although Israel had become a member of the United Nations on May 11, 1949, Jordan did not become a member until December 14, 1955. However, it was invited in 1949 to send a representative to make known to the Ad Hoc Political Committee its views on the Jerusalem question.

The U.S., the U.K., and France supported the Palestine Conciliation Commission's plan, rather than the Australian draft resolution. Even so, the French representative said his government really preferred full territorial internationalization and supported the Commission's compromise plan only because it felt that the U.N. was unwilling to undertake the responsibilities of full territorial internationalization, especially in view of the city's de facto partition.[21] Then, on November 28, the Lebanese representative, Dr. Charles Malik, made a stirring speech in the Ad Hoc Committee in which he expressed disappointment that France had not taken a bold stand on behalf of full territorial internationalization.[22] He asked if France had abandoned the historical rights which it had acquired in the Holy City in the course of centuries. He also wanted to know if the government and people of France were prepared to assume the responsibility before future generations for the fact that, faced with the opportunity to achieve peacefully the aims for which generations of Frenchmen had fought and died in Palestine for a thousand years, they were unable to rise to the occasion. This speech was to have its effect on France two days later.

The following day, the Ad Hoc Political Committee appointed a subcommittee composed of Australia, Canada, Cuba, Egypt, El Salvador, Greece, India, Iraq, Israel, Lebanon, Mexico, the Netherlands, Peru, Sweden, the Ukraine, the U.S.S.R., and Uruguay to study and report on the various proposals regarding Jerusalem. The Subcommittee approved the Soviet amendment calling on the Trusteeship Council to approve the draft statute for Jerusalem, and it incorporated this provision in the draft Australian resolution. While agreeing to eliminate the provision for a larger Palestine Conciliation Council to prepare a new plan for Jerusalem, it rejected the Soviet amendment which would dissolve the Commission. With a few other minor amendments, the Subcommittee adopted the Australian draft resolution and recommended it to the full Ad Hoc Political Committee.[23]

Territorial Internationalization
Reaffirmed

When the Subcommittee's report was taken up by the full Ad Hoc Political Committee, the Netherlands representative introduced a joint draft resolution proposed by the Netherlands and Sweden.[24] The Dutch-Swedish proposal called for functional internationalization of the Holy Places under the supervision of a United Nations commissioner responsible to the General Assembly and appointed by the Secretary General after nomination by a committee of the General Assembly to be composed of the eleven members of the Security Council. In introducing the draft resolution, the Netherlands representative said that in the view of his government it was better to adopt even an imperfect solution which was workable than to abide by an ideal solution which could not be carried out in practice. While the Subcommittee's draft resolution might be ideal, it was impossible to implement and maintain, he said; Jerusalem would be a small state surrounded by two larger states who were opposed to its creation and it would be inhabited by people who were opposed to the arrangement.

The Cuban representative seemed to favor the Palestine Conciliation Commission's plan, rather than the Subcommittee's plan, but he wanted to eliminate the possibility of any large measure of Soviet influence in Jerusalem, regardless of the plan adopted. Consequently, he introduced an amendment to the Subcommittee's draft resolution that would make the U.N. commissioner in Jerusalem responsible to the General Assembly rather than to the Trusteeship Council.[25] The Chairman of the Ad Hoc Political Committee ruled that the Cuban proposal was not an amendment but was in fact a separate resolution, and the Cuban representative accepted this decision.

The Bolivian representative also offered a draft resolution to rival the Subcommittee draft.[26] His proposal was for a form of functional internationalization with a juridical basis and called for the establishment of a commission which would formulate a draft statute for this purpose. The draft statute, he explained, might well follow the lines of the Headquarters Agreement between the U.N. and the U.S. Such an agreement between the U.N., Jordan, and Israel would confer a juridical status on the Holy Places and provide just those safeguards which the members of the U.N. desired. There was little interest in the Bolivian proposal and the Bolivian representative eventually withdrew it.

The French representative welcomed the Subcommittee's

report. He said he was glad that it had rejected the Palestine Conciliation Commission's proposal and had recommended the simpler, more radical solution which France favored.[27] As the Subcommittee had thus shown the determination of the United Nations to face the difficulties involved in establishing a *corpus separatum*, France would support the Subcommittee's draft resolution and it would assume its share of responsibility in the undertaking. The Egyptian representative also supported the Subcommittee's draft. He called attention to the Arab about-face and said he wished to emphasize the historic gesture being made by the Arabs, who for the first time were offering to relinquish in favor of the international community a city which had been committed to them as a sacred trust.[28] On the other hand, the Jordanian and Iraqi representatives rejected internationalization of any kind.[29] Israel once again rejected territorial internationalization and offered to accept a form of functional internationalization such as the Swedish and the Netherlands representatives proposed.[30]

The U.S. and U.K. representatives regretted that the Subcommittee had not taken seriously the Conciliation Commission's proposal, which they considered good.[31] They opposed the Subcommittee's draft resolution as impractical, and the U.S. representative, Mr. Ross, said that it would involve the Trusteeship Council in imposing on Jerusalem a system of government incompatible with the aspirations of its inhabitants. The Soviet representative, Mr. Tsarapkin, accused the U.S. and U.K. of conspiring to circumvent the 1947 partition plan.[32] He said that the U.S.S.R. would support the Subcommittee's draft resolution, which in the Soviet Union's view constituted the fairest and wisest solution to the Jerusalem question, and that any arrangement which perpetuated the division of the city between two rival forces would represent a serious danger to the peace of the area.

According to the Ad Hoc Political Committee's rules of procedure, the vote was taken first on the Subcommittee draft resolution, and it was adopted on December 7, 1949, by a vote of 35 to 13, with 11 abstentions.[33] The Swedish-Dutch draft resolution and the Cuban draft resolution were therefore not pressed to a vote. The Ad Hoc Political Committee submitted its report to the General Assembly, recommending the draft resolution for full territorial internationalization of Jerusalem.

The General Assembly took up the Ad Hoc Political Committee's report on December 8. Again terming the Ad Hoc Political Committee's draft resolution impractical, the Swedish and Netherlands representatives reintroduced their draft resolution in the Assembly.[34] The Swedish-Dutch proposal was immediately supported by Canada, Chile, Iceland, and Norway, and was preferred by the U.S. and the U.K. over the Ad Hoc Political Committee's draft resolution. The U.S. representative, Mr. Ross, said the Committee's draft resolution was a proposal to involve the U.N. in countless difficulties and responsibilities in order to achieve purposes not all of which were of genuine concern to the international community, such as the regulation of the continuing secular activities of the inhabitants of Jerusalem, both Arab and Jewish.[35] Further, the Ad Hoc Political Committee was proposing to establish a new and entirely separate political entity which did not conform to the wishes of the local population. Such a proposal would not result in the establishment of an international regime; it would merely result in further debate and would delay, perhaps finally postpone, the assumption by the United Nations of its rightful position in Jerusalem. The Soviet representative, Mr. Tsarapkin, charged that the U.S. and the U.K. had conspired to bring about the outbreak of the war in Palestine in order to restore British control through Jordanian King Abdallah.[36] It was for this reason, he said, that they sought to quash the internationalization effort and leave Abdallah in control of East Jerusalem. He urged support for the Ad Hoc Political Committee's draft resolution for full territorial internationalization.

Israel opposed the Ad Hoc Political Committee's draft resolution but was willing to go along with the Dutch-Swedish proposal.[37] The Syrian representative, Ahmad al-Shuqayri, and the Egyptian representative, Muhammad Kamil Abd al-Rahim Bey, again emphasized Arab magnanimity in now agreeing to lay down their sacred trust and permit the internationalization of Jerusalem.[38] Abd al-Rahim Bey said that as long as any part of Jerusalem was under Jewish control, the Arabs were threatened and the Holy Places were endangered. It was Israel, he said, that was obstructing the implementation of the U.N. decisions to internationalize the city. But, he explained, the U.N. need not be concerned by questions of practicality or impracticality. Echoing a persistent Arab refrain, he said that if the Great Powers sincerely supported internationalization, Israel would obey and everything would fall into place without difficulty. However, while the Syrian and Egyptian delegates were purporting to speak in the name of the Arabs, the Jordanian Foreign Minister sent a telegram to Secretary General Trygve Lie informing him that Jordan objected "to any measures and arrangments which may be taken" in regard to the internationalization of Jerusalem and would "oppose the execution of whatever is decided contrary to its rightful wishes."[39] The committee's draft resolution came to a vote on December 9 and was adopted by the General Assembly by a vote of 38 to 14, with 7 abstentions.[40] Those in favor included Lebanon, the Muslim countries, most of the Catholic countries, and all the Soviet bloc countries. The Swedish-Dutch resolution was not put to a vote.

Reaction to the General Assembly's action was not slow in coming. Abba Eban, Israel's delegate to the U.N., told the press in New York that "Israel does not have to bow to every resolution of the U.N. if it does not regard it as fair."[41] The following day, Vatican circles characterized the U.N. resolution as very satisfactory; but Acting Mayor Auster of West Jerusalem, borrowing a phrase from King Abdallah, said that the internationalization of Israeli-held Jerusalem by the U.N. could be carried out "only over our dead bodies."[42] The Knesset on December 13 approved a proposal by Prime Minister Ben-Gurion that it move to Jerusalem, despite a U.S. warning on December 12 to both Israel and Jordan that they should not undertake any actions that might imperil their future relations with the Vatican or the Arab states.[43] On December 14, Mr. Ben-Gurion made arrangements for the transfer of his office to Jerusalem and on December 16, he set January 1, 1950, as the deadline for the transfer of the rest of the government offices to Jerusalem, with the exception of the Ministries of Defense, Police, and Foreign Affairs.

King Abdallah notified the U.N. on December 10, 1949, that he was unalterably opposed to international control of Jerusalem. Up until August 1949, Abdallah had reportedly toyed with the idea of a joint kingdom with separate parliaments for the East and West Banks, but after the General Assembly's action in December 1949, he decided on a unified kingdom including Jordanian-held Jerusalem.[44] On December 13, he issued a decree dissolving the Jordanian Parliament as of January 1, 1950, and calling for elections throughout the kingdom.[45] Election day was set for April 11. Other published decrees, also dated December 13, amended the nationality law to confer Jordanian citizenship on the West Bankers and amended the electoral law to provide twenty seats in the Jordanian Parliament to represent the West Bank.[46]

A Statute for Jerusalem

The Trusteeship Council had already met in special session on December 8 to consider the question of the disposal of the former Italian colonies. Since the General Assembly resolution of December 9 called upon the Trusteeship Council to complete at its next session, whether regular or special, the preparation of the statute of Jerusalem, the Trusteeship Council added this item to the agenda of the special session on December 13. Israel and Jordan were at that time in the midst of their negotiations for a settlement and both were apprehensive lest the Trusteeship Council adopt a statute that might prejudice the arrangements they would make on Jerusalem. Consequently, the U.S. and the U.K. supported a Mexican suggestion in the Trusteeship Council that the matter not be discussed until after the turn of the year.[47] At the insistence of France and the U.S.S.R., however, the Council decided to begin discussions immediately.

The next several days were spent in the discussion of procedure and the type of changes that would have to be made in the draft statute to update it. Mexico suggested that Jordan and Israel be closely consulted in the preparation of the draft, warning that unless these two states accepted the statute, it would be a dead letter. The Mexican representative also suggested that, since Australia had initiated the General Assembly resolution reaffirming the call for the establishment of a *corpus separatum*, the Australian delegation might be invited to explain to the Council just how the resolution was to be implemented.[48] But Belgium objected to the notion of negotiating with Jordan and Israel, and the Iraqi representative, participating without vote in the discussion, said that if Jerusalem could not be Arab it should be international.[49] In his view, it was only Israel that was blocking internationalization and it would be a simple matter for the U.S. and the U.K. to make Israel bow to the decisions of the United Nations. On the substantive side, several representatives noted that the General Assembly's resolution called not only for the elimination of inapplicable provisions but for amendments in the direction of greater democratization.

Finally, on December 19, the Trusteeship Council adopted a resolution entrusting the Council President, Roger Garreau of France, with the task of submitting to it at the opening of the next regular session on January 19, 1950, a working paper to assist the Council in considering what revisions to make in the draft statute.[50] In order to satisfy those who wanted to consult with Israel and Jordan, the resolution also authorized the Council President to ascertain the views of interested governments, institutions, and organizations. Then, at the last meeting of the special session on December 20, the Council voted to ask Israel to revoke measures it had taken to transfer the government ministries and other offices to Jerusalem.[51]

The latter resolution did not have the desired effect. On December 26, the Israeli Knesset moved permanently to Jerusalem and on December 30, Abba Eban, Israel's delegate to the United Nations, addressed a letter to the U.N. Trusteeship Council rejecting the resolution of December 20. Then, on January 4, 1950, the General Zionist and Herut parties proposed in the Knesset a legislative act naming Jerusalem as the capital of Israel.[52] Prime Minister Ben-Gurion took the position that such an act was unnecessary, since Jerusalem had been made the capital by King David. Finally, a compromise was worked out and the Knesset adopted a resolution on January 23, 1950, proclaiming that Jerusalem had always been the capital of Israel.[53]

The Trusteeship Council convened again in regular session on January 19, but it was still seized with the problem of Italian Somaliland and it did not get around to considering the Council President's working paper on Jerusalem until January 30.[54] Mr. Garreau's paper called for division of the area of Jerusalem as defined in General Assembly resolutions of November 29, 1947, and December 9, 1949, into three zones:

(1) an Israeli zone consisting of most of the new city outside the walls, together with the train station and the railway to Tel Aviv; (2) a Jordanian zone consisting of the Muslim quarters of the Walled City, including the Haram al-Sharif, and the Wadi al-Jawz and Bab al-Zahira sections, the American Colony, and certain roads outside the walls; and (3) an international zone consisting of land taken in almost equal parts from the occupation zones defined by the Israeli-Jordanian armistice agreement to include all the Holy Places covered by the status quo of 1757. The international zone would be administered, under the supervision of the U.N.'s appointed governor of the Holy Places, by a municipal council elected by universal suffrage of the zone's inhabitants, regardless of nationality. The composition of the municipal council would be determined in such a manner as "to ensure equitable representation of the various religions."[55]

In presenting his plan, Mr. Garreau explained that he was specifying what should be excluded from the international zone rather than what was to be included in it.[56] He noted, for example, that almost the whole of the new city outside the walls was excluded. The Muslim district and the Haram al-Sharif in the Walled City would be excluded, since those areas were already administered by a Muslim state. The Amman-Nablus highway which passed beneath the walls would remain under the authority of Jordan, since it was the only road from Amman to northern Palestine in reasonably good condition at the moment. On the other hand, the Armenian, Christian, and Jewish districts of the Walled City would be included in the international zone, the boundaries of which could only be established on the spot.

As enclosures to his report, Mr. Garreau submitted a statement by the Greek Orthodox Archbishop in North and South America on behalf of the Orthodox Patriarchate of Jerusalem, a statement by Bishop Tiran Nersoyan (Primate of the Armenian Apostolic Orthodox Church of America) on behalf of the Armenian Patriarchate of Jerusalem, a statement by the Director of the Commission of the Churches on International Affairs, and a statement by an unofficial fact-finding mission of the American Christian Palestine Committee. These statements were repeated again in person before the Trusteeship Council during the first ten days of February. The representatives of the Orthodox and Armenian Patriarchates of Jerusalem favored full territorial internationalization of the whole city along the lines of the 1947 partition plan. The representative from the American Christian Palestine Committee opposed full territorial internationalization and urged the establishment of a U.N. commission entrusted with supervision of the Holy Places. The representative of the Commission of the Churches on International Affairs said that, while the churches and religious organizations were generally agreed that some form of internationalization was necessary, their opinions ranged from advocacy of complete international jurisdiction to that of a very small degree of international responsibility. He called the Council's attention to the plan put forth by the Archbishop of Canterbury on October 31, 1949, but noted that after the General Assembly had reaffirmed on December 9 the provisions of the 1947 partition plan referring to Jerusalem, the Archbishop had endorsed the General Assembly's action.

The Orthodox Patriarchate, mindful of the frequent efforts of the Palestinian Arabs to break the exclusive Greek hold on the Patriarchate, also wanted a provision in the statute to prevent lay interference in the administration of religious institutions, particularly monastic organizations.[57] Bishop Nersoyan, appearing on behalf of the Armenian Patriarchate, suggested that the legislative council of the internationalized city be bicameral, with an elective lower house and an appointed upper house.[58] Each of the two houses would have a membership composed of equal numbers of Christians, Muslims, and Jews.

On February 10, 1950, the Trusteeship Council shelved the Garreau plan and adopted a Chinese draft resolution calling for immediate consideration of the 1948 draft statute.[59] The following day, the Council voted to invite Jordan and Israel to send representatives to state the views of their respective governments on the revision of the draft statute and its implementation. Representatives of both Jordan and Israel appeared before the Council on February 20. The Jordanian representative simply stated that his government's attitude remained unchanged and that it would not enter into any discussion on the internationalization of Jerusalem.[60]

The Israeli representative, Abba Eban, said that the idea

that any regime imposed for the sake of religious interests could flourish or endure in the presence of an aggrieved, disaffected, and turbulent population must be rejected as a self-evident fallacy.[61] He observed that the religious life of Jerusalem could be serene only if the city were politically content. Since the question of implementation was so powerfully affected by the factor of consent, it was his duty frankly to describe Jewish feelings, both in Jerusalem and in the remainder of Israel, as being opposed to the draft statute under discussion. He said that Israel sympathized with the desire of the Council to provide protection for the Holy Places. He pointed out that according to U.N. Map Number 229 (November 1949) the Holy Places all lay within an area of one and a half square miles, but that the draft statute would internationalize an area of approximately one hundred square miles. He reminded the Trusteeship Council that Israel had proposed during the third session of the General Assembly that international control be confined either to the Holy Places themselves or to that area within historic Jerusalem in which the Holy Places were situated.

Eban said that Israel still stood ready to conclude agreements with the U.N. for the international control of the Holy Places. He noted, however, that the majority of the U.N. members preferred a statutory arrangement rather than a contractual arrangement. Hence, while Israel opposed territorial internationalization of West Jerusalem, it would be prepared to participate in the preparation of a statute for the Holy Places which would spring from the authority of the U.N. itself and not be in the form of a contract between the U.N. and the occupying powers. Instead of an accredited representative of the U.N. in Jerusalem as proposed by Israel in its draft resolution in the Ad Hoc Political Committee in the fourth session of the General Assembly in the fall of 1949, Mr. Eban proposed that U.N. representation be established in Jerusalem as a result of the right of the world community to indicate in this manner its interest in the Holy City. This representation would be wholly separate from the occupying states and would be a sovereign authority of the U.N. The U.N. representative would have full control of the Holy Places, including protection, free access, and repairs. Israel was even prepared to concede a certain degree of extraterritoriality as far as the Holy Places were concerned. The U.N. representative would have the sole power of decision in disputes between the different religious communities in Jerusalem. Thus, insofar as the Holy Places were concerned, the authority of the occupying government would more or less be withdrawn.

The Belgian representative was impressed by Eban's observation that the portion of Jerusalem which held the Holy Places had an area of only one and a half square miles while the area covered by the draft statute was approximately one hundred square miles.[62] He suggested that the area to be covered by the statute be reduced, but the other members of the Council objected on the grounds that the Trusteeship Council was an executive organ and obligated to carry out the instructions of the General Assembly whether the Council agreed with them or not. The General Assembly resolution of December 9, 1949, had defined the area to be included in the *corpus separatum*. With this matter settled, there was no further attempt to depart seriously from the 1948 draft statute except in the composition of the legislative council.

As in 1948, the composition of the legislative council was a major problem. On February 27, the French representative put forth again the proposal, previously made in the Trusteeship Council in 1948, that the legislative council be divided equally among Jews, Muslims, and Christians.[63] On March 7 he said that he would shortly make an additional proposal which would be responsive to the suggestions of the Armenian Patriarchate that the legislative council include members appointed by the religious authorities in Jerusalem.[64] Seeing the possibility of a legislative council dominated by a Christian-Muslim alliance, the Iraqi representative waxed lyrical about the French formula and said that acceptance of the principle of equal participation would constitute a great sacrifice which the Muslim world was prepared to make for the sake of establishing Jerusalem as an international city—a city which had for centuries been ruled by Muslims.[65] The following day, the French representative introduced his new proposal, calling for a legislative council composed of 37 members.[66] Twenty-five of these would be elected by four electoral colleges: eight each by Muslim, Jewish, and Christian electoral colleges and one by a mixed college composed of residents of Jerusalem who declare that they do not wish to register with any of the other three colleges. The other twelve members would be appointed in equal numbers by the religious authorities of the Christian, Muslim, and Jewish communities. After amending it to raise the number of appointed members to a maximum of 15, the Council adopted the French proposal.

The Trusteeship Council also made changes in the immigration provisions of the statute. Under the 1948 draft statute, provision was made for unrestricted immigration from the Jewish and Arab states in Palestine. Under the 1950 statute, all immigration was made dependent on the absorptive capacity of the *corpus separatum* and the "maintenance of equality between the various communities."[67] The Trusteeship Council reserved to itself the authority to issue instructions to the governor on immigration. Other major changes were the elimination of the article providing for inclusion of Jerusalem in an economic union with an Arab and a Jewish state in a partitioned Palestine, the inclusion of a provision for return of refugees to Jerusalem, the addition of provisions allowing the governor to exchange representatives with foreign states, and the inclusion of a provision for the return of religious properties seized without equitable compensation since the outbreak of World War II to their original owners or, if this were not possible, for their transfer to another religious organization of the same confession. This last provision, suggested by the U.S., was intended to cover the problem of German Lutheran property seized by the mandatory power during World War II.

Notwithstanding its illiberal actions on the legislative council and immigration, the Council showed some sensitivity to the charge that the 1948 statute had not been sufficiently democratic. The requirement that the governor and the members of the special police force not be nationals of Jerusalem, Israel, or the Arab state in Palestine was removed. The authority to approve a flag, a seal, and a coat of arms for Jerusalem was vested in the legislative council, rather than the Trusteeship Council. Minor restrictions were placed on the authority of the governor to legislate.

Stalemate

The Trusteeship Council approved the statute on April 4, 1950, and requested the Council President to transmit the text of the statute to Jordan and Israel with a request for their full cooperation in implementing it. Mr. Garreau transmitted the text to Jordan and Israel on April 6 and requested them to send a representative to Athens to discuss its implementation with him on April 17. Jordan did not reply but proceeded with its elections on April 11, and on April 24 the new Parliament gave formal approval to the union of the East Bank and the West Bank, including Jerusalem.[68] The U.K. announced on April 27 its formal recognition of the Jordanian union and at the same time extended de jure recognition to Israel.* But in view of the U.N. resolutions on Jerusalem, the U.K. made it clear that it was according only de facto recognition to the partition of Jerusalem between Israel and Jordan.

The Israeli Foreign Minister, Moshe Sharett, agreed to discuss the statute with Garreau but proposed that he come to Tel Aviv. The Council President accepted Sharett's invitation on condition that Jordan also be willing to discuss the statute. However, in the absence of a reply from Jordan, Garreau abandoned his plan to go to Tel Aviv on the grounds that discussion with only one of the parties was not practical. Further talks did take place in New York between the Israeli representative and the Council President, and on May 26 Eban sent Garreau a memorandum setting forth Israel's views. Israel saw no good reason for internationalizing the portion of Jerusalem under Israeli control. The memorandum pointed out that scarcely a house or a street in the Israeli part of Jerusalem existed prior to 1860. Only two of the more than thirty sites marked as Holy Places in the authorized map prepared for the Trusteeship Council were situated within the Israeli zone of Jerusalem and these were at the very edge of West Jerusalem.[69]

The memorandum also directed severe criticism at the statute itself:

> Thus, the implementation of the Statute would involve the United Nations in the process of destroying free and stable democratic institutions in Jerusalem as a prelude to the imposition, against the popular will, of an authoritarian regime introduced from outside.... Implementation of the Statute

*The U.S. extended de jure recognition to Jordan and Israel on January 31, 1949. The U.S. took no formal notice of the unification in 1950 of the East and West Banks of the Jordan.

88

would have drastic effect on the life of every man and woman in Jewish Jerusalem. . . . From having complete control of the life of the New City which they had built and defended with their own hands, the Jewish population would be reduced to the level of having no power or authority whatever in the affairs of Jerusalem. For, under the operation of the Statute, the Jews of the New City, who form the considerable majority of the entire population of Jerusalem, would now have less than one-third of the representation in an impotent and uninfluential "Legislative Council" (article 21). . . . Their lives would suddenly become subject to the arbitrary enactments of a constitution which was neither formulated by them nor evolved out of their consent and experience. For the Statute itself, with its omnipotent Governor and its artificially constituted Legislative Council, is modelled precisely on the absolutist forms of government which used to be applied in backward regions in the days before the elementary principle of self-government began to secure a foothold even in the dependent areas of the world.[70]

Eban's memorandum also criticized the article on immigration (article 30): "A *numerus clausus*, reminiscent of the practices of racial discrimination, would prevent the Jews of Israel from taking up residence in the very City which the Jewish people immortalized in this history of mankind."[71] But, having said this, Eban reiterated Israel's proposal for functional international control of the Holy Places. Garreau reported to the Trusteeship Council on June 2, 1950, his conclusion that implementation of the statute would seem in the circumstances to be seriously compromised. On June 14, the Council decided to submit its report to the General Assembly without taking any further steps in the matter.

On April 17, 1950—the very day set by Garreau for a meeting with the Israeli and Jordanian representatives in Athens—the U.S.S.R. had informed the U.N. Secretary General that it was withdrawing its support for the resolution of December 9, 1949. This Soviet move was not inconsistent with the stand of the U.S.S.R. throughout the Palestine crisis of 1947-1949. It had supported the Palestine partition plan and the establishment of Israel as a means of removing British influence from that area of the Near East. It had seen the failure of the Arab state to come into being and the subsequent Arab military action against Israel as part of a design by the U.K. and the

U.S. to restore British influence in Palestine. During the debate in the General Assembly in 1949 on the Jerusalem question, the Soviet delegate had hurled his barbs not at Israel but at Jordan, the U.K., and the U.S., and had accused King Abdallah of being a British stooge. Once the General Assembly had reaffirmed its preference for territorial internationalization of Jerusalem and had thus set Israel (and Jordan) at complete variance with the U.N. and the Western powers, the U.S.S.R. saw no further need to support internationalization. This attitude was already evident in the fact that the U.S.S.R. took no part in the Trusteeship Council meetings at which the statute was completed and approved. The notification on April 17 to the Secretary General simply formalized an already existing situation.

The defection of the U.S.S.R. from the Communist-Catholic-Arab coalition did not strengthen the hand of the functionalists, but it did weaken the territorialist camp. In the General Assembly in 1950, the result was a stalemate. The Trusteeship Council had declined to take further steps toward implementation of the statute without further instructions from the General Assembly. When the matter came up in the Ad Hoc Political Committee in December 1950, Sweden introduced again its proposal for functional internationalization.[72] Representing the territorialists, Belgium introduced a proposal for the appointment of a four-man commission to negotiate with Israel and Jordan on a solution "in accordance with the principles already adopted by the General Assembly."[73] As was to be expected, the U.S., the U.K., the Netherlands, and Denmark were among those who supported the Swedish proposal and expressed the view that territorial internationalization would be unacceptable to the inhabitants and would thus be undemocratic. The Labour Government in Australia had been defeated on December 10, 1949, and Australia now joined the ranks of the functionalists.

Israel accepted the Swedish proposal but Jordan opposed it at first, contending that it would derogate from Jordanian sovereignty and reflect adversely on Jordan's administration of East Jerusalem and on Jordan's past conduct, which had been that of fairness and tolerance for all religions.* After the

---

*Jordan, not yet a member of the United Nations, was invited to send a representative to express its views on the Jerusalem question.

Swedish proposal was amended at the suggestion of the U.K., the U.S., and Uruguay so as to remove provisions that seem to call into question Israeli and Jordanian sovereignty, the Jordanian representative said the proposal was acceptable. Like Israel, Jordan opposed the Belgian proposal on the grounds that it would alienate, denationalize, and disenfranchise the inhabitants of Jerusalem. In addition, the Jordanian representative pointed out that territorial internationalization of Jerusalem would have the effect of severing all existing land routes between the area south of Bethlehem and the rest of the kingdom. The other Arab representatives opposed the Swedish draft resolution and insisted that only full internationalization would bring permanent stability and prevent the clash of the two authorities currently occupying Jerusalem. The U.S.S.R. said that any just solution must take into account the interests of the Jewish and Arab inhabitants of the city. Because the resolutions of 1948 and 1949 calling for internationalization were not satisfactory to either, it could no longer support these resolutions. The U.S.S.R. considered both the Swedish and the Belgian resolutions unsatisfactory and therefore abstained from voting for either of them.

Since only a majority vote is needed in the Ad Hoc Political Committee, the Belgian draft resolution was adopted by a vote of 30 in favor, 18 against, and 11 abstentions.[74] But in the General Assembly, a two-thirds vote is required on important matters, and the resolution was not adopted when it came to a vote on December 15.[75] The General Assembly ended without a resolution. The Assembly discussed the matter again in 1952, but it still took no action.

Chapter 6

Reunification

Diplomatic Problems

The stalemate produced in the General Assembly in 1950 lasted almost 17 years. In the meantime, the Israel-Jordan negotiations foundered. Jerusalem remained partitioned along the lines of the cease-fire agreements of 1949, and both Jordan and Israel took measures to strengthen their hold on their portions of the city. The Western powers protested to both sides on such actions as tended to prejudice a settlement along lines adopted by the United Nations. In making such protests, the U.S. and the U.K. based their stand not on the premise that territorial internationalization was necessarily the best solution for Jerusalem but on the grounds that the resolutions of November 29, 1947, December 11, 1948, and December 9, 1949, were the last actions by the U.N. on the matter and should therefore be respected. The U.S.S.R., even before its withdrawal of support for internationalization, was not bothered by such scruples. For example, when the Israel Constituent Assembly opened in Jerusalem on February 14, 1949, Russian Minister Pavel Yershov attended the formal opening, while the U.S., U.K., and French representatives stayed away.

The most active problem connected with the Jerusalem question after the partition of the city stemmed from the transfer by Israel of its seat of government to West Jerusalem. In fact, continued and vociferous Arab League protests against this Israeli action diverted attention from Jordanian actions and made it appear that Israel was the sole obstacle to a Jerusalem settlement. As we have seen, the government moved to Jerusalem in December 1949 and on January 23, 1950, the Knesset proclaimed that Jerusalem had always been the capital. Only three Ministries were left in Tel Aviv: the Ministry of Defense, for security reasons; the Ministry of Police, for convenience; and the Ministry for Foreign Affairs, because most of the foreign embassies were situated there. In addition, President Weizmann, who lived in Rechovot, maintained his office in Tel Aviv.

As long as the Ministry for Foreign Affairs and the President's office were in Tel Aviv, the foreign embassies had little difficulty in avoiding going to Jerusalem to deal with the Israeli Government. But President Weizmann died on November 9, 1952, and he was succeeded by Yitzhak Ben-Zvi, a longtime resident of Jerusalem. President Ben-Zvi transferred his office to Jerusalem, and the question soon arose as to where foreign ambassadors were to present their letters of credence. The first emissary to present his letters of credence in Jerusalem was the Netherlands Minister, G. W. Boissevain, on May 4, 1953. This presented no problem, however, since the Netherlands had established its legation in Jerusalem. Later in the year, the representative of Chile followed Boissevain's example. The first envoy of a big power to go to Jerusalem for this purpose was the Russian Minister, Alexander Abramov, who presented his credentials to President Ben-Zvi on December 4, 1953.[1] A problem arose when the new Italian Minister arrived on December 2, 1953, because his government would not permit him to go to Jerusalem for the presentation. He was finally allowed to present his credentials in Tiberias on December 16, 1953, but he was the last to present his credentials outside Jerusalem. The Israeli Government made it clear that in the future it would not accept envoys if they did not present their credentials in Jerusalem.[2] British Ambassador John Nichols presented his credentials in Jerusalem on November 10, 1954; and U.S. Ambassador Edward P. Lawson presented his credentials there two days later.[3] In response to protests by the Arab ambassadors, U.S. Secretary of State John Foster Dulles said that Lawson's presentation of credentials in Jerusalem had nothing to do with U.S. policy on Jerusalem and that the U.S. continued to support the U.N. resolutions.[4] The British Foreign Office took a similar stand.[5]

The transfer of the Ministry for Foreign Affairs to Jerusalem on July 13, 1953, presented more serious difficulties for foreign embassies in Israel. On May 4, 1952, the Israeli Government announced that the Ministry would move to Jerusalem as soon as technical arrangements could be made. It was explained that it was too inconvenient to have the Ministry for Foreign Affairs cut off from the Prime Minister and other government departments. Nevertheless, the major Western governments protested.[6] The Israeli Government waited until after the seventh session of the General Assembly in the fall of 1952. Noting that it, like the two previous sessions, had passed without any further resolutions on Jerusalem, Israel decided that the move could be made without serious repercussion. Consequently, on July 10, 1953, the Ministry for Foreign Affairs informed the diplomatic corps that it would begin operations in Jerusalem on July 13. Again the Western powers protested.

For a number of months after the move, contact between the Foreign Ministry and the foreign embassies in Tel Aviv was of the most tenuous sort. The embassies considered the Foreign Ministry "off-limits," but ambassadors and ministers managed to see Foreign Minister Sharett on weekends at his home in Ramat Gan, a suburb of Tel Aviv. Correspondence with the Foreign Ministry was directed to the Liaison Office which the Ministry had left behind in Tel Aviv for that purpose.[7] The break in the diplomatic boycott of the Foreign Ministry came on December 2, 1953, when the newly arrived Soviet Minister, Mr. Abramov, became the first envoy to call on the Foreign Minister in Jerusalem.* The other envoys did not immediately emulate Abramov, but when Sharett became Prime Minister as well as Foreign Minister on January 26, 1954, they adopted the practice of calling on him in Jerusalem in his capacity as Prime Minister. Diplomats other than the chiefs of missions began calling during this period at the Foreign Ministry. When Sharett ceded the Prime Ministry to Ben-Gurion in November 1955 and kept only the portfolio of Foreign Minister, he adopted the practice of going to Tel Aviv once a week to receive envoys in the Liaison Office. But from that time on, envoys called on the Foreign Minister in Jerusa-

*The New West Times, December 3, 1953. The U.S.S.R. had broken relations with Israel on February 12, 1953, following the explosion of a bomb in the garden of the Soviet Legation in Tel Aviv on the evening of February 9. Several people, including the Soviet Minister's wife, were injured. Although Israel apologized immediately and offered compensation, the U.S.S.R. held Israel responsible and severed relations. Agreement on the resumption of relations was reached in July 1953, and the new Soviet Minister arrived in Israel at the end of November 1953.

94

lem if it was necessary to see him at any time other than the one day he went to Tel Aviv each week. The boycott gradually withered away and on July 6, 1962, the Foreign Ministry gave notice that for budgetary reasons, the Liaison Office in Tel Aviv would be closed on July 15. The foreign embassies protested. The U.S. made clear that any accommodation made by its embassy should not be construed as affecting or implying any change in U.S. attitude concerning the status of Jerusalem. Other embassies made the same point.

After the transfer of the Foreign Ministry to Jerusalem, Israel urged other countries to establish their diplomatic representation in Jerusalem. The Netherlands Legation was already there, since the Netherlands Representative for Palestine and Jordan had simply remained in Jerusalem after the establishment of the state of Israel and had been accredited as Minister to the government of Israel in February 1949 while the government was still in Tel Aviv. Greece established a diplomatic representative in Jerusalem. Guatemala and Uruguay soon established their legations there. When the Netherlands and Israel raised their legations to embassy level on January 14, 1958, the Netherlands became the first state to have its embassy in Jerusalem. By 1967, nearly forty per cent of the 54 foreign diplomatic establishments in Israel were located in Jerusalem.[8] Most of these were Latin American and African embassies. In fact, two-thirds of the Latin American countries represented in Israel had their embassies in Jerusalem.

The Holy Places and Religious Affairs during the Partition

Respect for the Holy Places, which had been the avowed concern of the world in 1947, proved to be less of a problem than had been anticipated. On the Israeli side, the sanctity of Christian shrines was scrupulously observed. Occasional acts of vandalism in Christian cemeteries in Jerusalem were officially frowned on and the courts also viewed them seriously. When charges of proselytizing were leveled at Christian schools in Jerusalem in late 1962 and early 1963, and serious acts of vandalism were directed at these schools, the courts dealt sternly with the vandals, including the sons of several Knesset members. Perhaps the most serious incident in connection with the last mentioned events was the sorry spectacle to which the world was treated when, on January 24, 1963, the Minister for Religious Affairs, Zerah Wahrhaftig, addressed the foundation meeting in Tel Aviv of the Council to Combat the Missions.[9] The Israeli populace, however, paid little heed to the fears voiced by the Minister and a few fanatics that Christianity was about to sweep the country and the issue quickly faded away.

On the Jordan side, there was likewise little problem over the Christian Holy Places. King Abdallah appointed Raghib al-Nashashibi Pasha on January 5, 1951, as the first Guardian of the Haram al-Sharif and Supreme Custodian of the Holy Places.[10] When Raghib Pasha died on April 10, 1951, Husayn Fakhri al-Khalidi was appointed on April 19, 1951, to take his place. One of the outstanding achievements during the Jordanian period was the agreement reached on June 27, 1961, by the Orthodox, Latins, and Armenians, with Jordanian Government assistance, to carry out the necessary repairs to the Church of the Holy Sepulchre. This was an issue that had been pending for a number of years.

Perhaps the most serious difficulty connected with the Holy Places was the question of the Jewish Holy Places in Jordanian hands. Although Article VIII of the Israel-Jordanian Armistice Agreement[11] provided for free access by Israeli Jews to the Wailing Wall, Jordan refused to implement this provision. In addition, the shrine of Simon the Just was neglected; a road was constructed through the Jewish cemetery on the Mount of Olives; and it was later discovered after Israel captured the Jordanian portion of the city that headstones from Jewish graves had been used for construction purposes, some of them in footpaths to army latrines.[12] On the other hand, Jordan periodically charged that Israel was desecrating the Mamilla Muslim cemetery in West Jerusalem.

Like the Mandatory Government, the Jordanian Government found it necessary to intervene in some of the internal Christian disputes. The most serious of these was in the Armenian Patriarchate in Jerusalem after the death of Patriarch Guregh Israelian on October 28, 1949. The monastic Brotherhood of St. James in Jerusalem elects the Patriarch under authority derived from the Armenian National Constitution promulgated in 1863 by the Ottoman Porte.[13] When Patriarch Guregh died the Brotherhood was torn between two rival groups: the Tashnaqs, who, because they were anti-Soviet, refused to recognize the authority of the Katholikos of Echmiadzin in Soviet Armenia and looked instead to the Katholikos of Sis in Antilyas, Lebanon, for spiritual guidance; and the anti-Tashnaqs, who continued to accept the Katholikos of Echmiadzin as the supreme authority in the Church. The Brotherhood was able to install pro-Tashnaq Archbishop Yeghishe Derderian as Locum Tenens until a new Patriarch could be elected. Derderian aspired to be Patriarch, but his rival was the anti-Tashnaq Primate of the Armenian Apostolic Orthodox Church of America, Tiran Nersoyan, who had become an archbishop in 1951. Many suspected that Derderian was delaying the call for an election until he could assure himself of victory. In 1955 Nersoyan retired as Primate in America and returned to Jerusalem, but on October 9, 1956, the Jordanian Government deported him on the grounds that he was engaged in communist activity.[14] The Brotherhood suspected that Derderian was behind the deportation and it reacted by deposing Derderian as Locum Tenens on October 13 and electing Nersoyan in his stead.[15] National elections were held in Jordan on October 21, 1956, and the new Prime Minister, Sulayman al-Nabulsi, reversed the deportation order of the previous cabinet. Nersoyan returned in triumph on November 15, 1956.

Derderian replied to this series of events by initiating a suit in the Jordanian High Court to prevent Nersoyan from being elected Patriarch.[16] The Court ruled in mid-March 1957 that it was not competent to entertain the suit, and Nersoyan was elected Patriarch on March 20, 1957. This brought another suit by Derderian on the same day.[17] The case dragged through the courts until it was finally decided in Nersoyan's favor on December 5, 1957, and on December 7, Patriarch-elect Nersoyan applied for the customary formal recognition by the king. But the Nabulsi Government had fallen on April 14, 1957, and the government of Ibrahim Hashim responded by issuing a deportation order against him. An appeal to the king brought a stay of deportation on February 4, 1958. Then, on August 30, 1958, Nersoyan was seized while participating in a religious procession and deported for the second time.[18] Nersoyan resigned in early 1960 as Patriarch-elect. The

Brotherhood was enlarged by the addition of six new members, and in June 1960, Derderian was elected Patriarch. The anti-Derderian forces intitiated a suit in the courts, but King Husayn, no doubt preferring a pro-Tashnaq Patriarch, settled the issue by formally recognizing Derderian as Patriarch on August 10, 1960. The enthronement took place on August 21, 1960.

The Jordanian Government also found itself involved in the struggle between the Arabizers and the Hellenizers in the Orthodox Patriarchate, and in this case, the Arabizers almost succeeded in achieving all their goals. When the Patriarch Timotheos died on December 31, 1955, the Orthodox laity sought to delay the election of a new Patriarch until they could win the reforms they desired. Draft legislation was drawn up that would (1) give the laity a voice in the financial affairs of the Patriarchate, (2) provide that in order to be eligible to be Patriarch, the candidate must be a Jordanian citizen and must be able to read and write perfect Arabic, and (3) require that, in order to be a bishop or priest, a person must be a citizen of Jordan or another Arab state and must be able to read and write Arabic well. The Jordanian Cabinet under Prime Minister Nabulsi approved the draft law on December 23, 1956, and the lay leaders were so confident of the law's passage through Parliament that they withdrew their objections to the patriarchal election. The Patriarch Benedictos was elected on January 29, 1957.[19] His election was recognized by King Husayn on February 21, 1957, and he was enthroned on March 1, 1957.[20]

Meanwhile, the draft law on the Orthodox Patriarchate was passed by the Jordanian House of Representatives and was referred to the Senate. The Senate made several amendments and referred it back to the lower house on February 18, 1957. Since the amendments were minor, it was generally assumed that the draft law would sail through the House of Representatives. But as soon as the new Patriarch was enthroned, he began lobbying against it, and the draft law was pigeonholed in the House during the rest of 1957. In 1958 Jordan had a new Prime Minister, Ibrahim Hashim, and the Cabinet on April 7, 1958, submitted to the Parliament a new draft law on the Orthodox Patriarchate. The new draft eliminated the provisions for a lay voice in the financial affairs of the Patriarchate which were in the draft law in 1957. However, Patriarch

Benedictos reportedly opposed even this draft, and it was allowed to die quietly in the Legal Committee in the House of Representatives. Then, as a gesture to the Arab laity, Patriarch Benedictos consecrated Simon Gharafeh as Bishop of Jerash on August 6, 1960. Bishop Gharafeh was thus the first Arab bishop in Jordan belonging to the Orthodox Patriarchate in Jerusalem in modern times.

Another Christian controversy in which the Jordanian Government became involved was the dispute between the Abyssinians and the Copts over the ownership of the monastery of Dayr al-Sultan, adjacent to the Church of the Holy Sepulchre on the east side. The monastery is occupied by Abyssinian monks under a Coptic guardian, but the Copts insist that the Abyssinians living there do so as their guests and on their sufferance.[21] In 1961, a Jordanian ministerial council conducted an inquiry and decided that the monastery belonged to the Abyssinians. The Copts, working through their Patriarch in Alexandria, persuaded the U.A.R. Government to intervene on their behalf and the Jordanian Government reversed its decision.[22]

The Israeli Capture of East Jerusalem

The Jerusalem question gradually slipped into the background after 1953. Jordan declared in 1960 that Jerusalem was one of the two capitals of the Kingdom, and the Western powers duly protested.* But the partition of Jerusalem was an established, if not a legal, fact of life. Neither Jordan nor Israel was particularly dissatisfied. If Israel had designs on East Jerusalem it was certainly not apparent, and during the outbreak of hostilities between Israel and Egypt in October 1956, the armistice line between Israel and Jordan remained quiet. Israeli Government spokesmen repeatedly said that, when the time was ripe, Israel would ask the U.N. to revise its position on Jerusalem. Israel probably hoped also that one day the question of access to the Wailing Wall would be successfully resolved.

*This was in reality a reaffirmation of a similar declaration on July 27, 1953, when the Jordanian Cabinet met in Jerusalem for the first time. See *The New York Times*, July 28, 1953. The text of the U.S. note of protest, dated April 5, 1960, may be found in Marjorie Whiteman, *Digest of International Law*, Vol. I, p. 594.

This situation was to change abruptly in 1967 as the culmination of a chain of events beginning in 1965. Al-Fatah, an Arab guerrilla organization, began a campaign of sabotage in Israel in January 1965.† As the activities of the organization grew over the months, it became increasingly evident that it was directed from bases in Syria and sentiment grew in Israel, especially in military circles, for a strike against the main bases of al-Fatah. Arab apprehension in Jordan and Syria rose, since these two countries were most likely to receive the brunt of Israeli retaliation. The Jordanian Government took steps to prevent its territory from being used to provide transit points for al-Fatah members passing from Syria to Israel. While the Syrian official radio broadcast the boastful and exaggerated communiques of al-Fatah, the Syrian Government disclaimed any responsibility for al-Fatah's activities and proclaimed an inability to do anything about the organization.

The U.S.S.R. sought to capitalize on the rising tension to direct Arab hostility against the U.S. Soviet strategy in the Near East had undergone a shift in the mid-1950's, after the death of Stalin; the new Soviet leadership reversed the policy of refusing to cooperate with bourgeois nationalists and decided to exploit neutralist sentiment in the Near East. In view of Israel's apparent drift toward abandonment of its avowed policy of non-identification and its increasing identification with the Western camp, the Arabs, notably Egypt, appeared to furnish a better vehicle for furthering the Soviet aim of ridding the area of Western influence. In the spring of 1966, Soviet propaganda charged that the CENTO Foreign Ministers meeting in Ankara and the U.S. Chiefs of Mission Conference in Beirut in April 1966 had as their purpose the planning and coordination of a joint U.S.-Israel plan for an Israeli attack on Syria. The visit of the U.S. Sixth Fleet to Beirut, which coincided with the Chiefs of Mission Conference, was cited as part of the plot. Then, on May 25, 1966, while Premier Kosygin was on a visit to the U.A.R., the Soviet Foreign Ministry summoned the Israeli Ambassador in Moscow and handed him a statement, described as the harshest in ten years, in which the U.S.S.R. accused Israel of massing troops on the

†The official name of this organization in Arabic is Fath. Since the form "al-Fatah" is more familiar to Western readers, it is used here for convenience.

border of Syria and plotting with the imperialists against Syria.[23] Israel refuted the charges in a statement handed to Soviet Ambassador Chuvakhin on June 2, 1966.

Having obtained considerable mileage out of the charges of a plot against Syria in the spring of 1966, the U.S.S.R. apparently decided to try a similar gambit in 1967. The occasion was furnished by a statement made by Israeli Prime Minister Levi Eshkol in early May 1967 that Israel's patience with the activities of al-Fatah was growing thin. Arab nerves were frayed as a result of a large-scale Israeli retaliatory raid into Jordan in November 1966, the reaction to which almost resulted in King Husayn's loss of his throne. Tension was further heightened in April 1967 by an incident between Israel and Syria. Israeli aircraft knocked out Syrian gun positions that had been shelling Israeli villages, and shot down six Syrian airplanes. Then, on May 13, 1967, the U.S.S.R. supplied false intelligence to Syria and the U.A.R. to the effect that Israel was concentrating on the Syrian armistice line from eleven to thirteen brigades and that Israel would attack Syria on May 17.[24] The Arab reaction was probably greater than the U.S.S.R. expected and certainly was in excess of the reaction of the previous year. The U.A.R. and Syria consulted immediately. U.A.R. President Nasser ordered some 50,000 Egyptian troops into Sinai, bringing the total number of troops facing Israel to 80,000. He also requested that the United Nations Emergency Force, placed in the Gaza Strip and along the Egyptian side of the Egyptian-Israel armistice line in 1957, be withdrawn. Encouraged by the enthusiastic Arab response, he subsequently proclaimed a blockade of the Strait of Tiran. Israel, most of whose oil supply passes through the strait to the port of Eilat, had warned that such a blockade would be a *casus belli* and consequently it struck at the U.A.R. on June 5.

King Husayn of Jordan had signed a joint defense agreement with the U.A.R. in Cairo on May 30 and, despite an appeal from Israel not to enter the war,[25] Jordan, like Syria, came to the U.A.R.'s assistance. In Jerusalem, the fighting began with Jordan's attempt to seize Government House from the U.N. Because of its high and strategic location between East and West Jerusalem, possession of Government House would give its occupant a distinct advantage in any attempt to dominate the rest of the city. The Israelis promptly pushed the Jordanians out and, circling the Walled City, they entered it from the east through St. Stephen's gate. By the time of the cease-fire on June 10, Israel had occupied East Jerusalem, the West Bank of the Jordan, the Gaza Strip, the Sinai Peninsula, and the Golan Heights in Syria.

The cease-fire having been achieved, the United Nations next turned to the problem of a solution for the crisis. The Arabs, supported by the U.S.S.R. and the communist countries of Eastern Europe except Romania, were demanding Israeli withdrawal to the positions occupied on June 4.[26] East Jerusalem was to be restored to Jordan. Israeli Prime Minister Eshkol, on the other hand, announced in the Knesset on June 12 that Israel believed that the previous armistice regimes had been overtaken and that a new situation now prevailed in the Near East.[27] In these circumstances, Israel would not withdraw from the occupied territories without a formal peace with the Arab states. The U.S. position was announced by President Johnson in a speech on June 19 in which he listed five fundamental principles for peace in the Near East: (1) the fundamental right of every nation in the area to exist and to have this right respected by its neighbors; (2) justice for the refugees; (3) respect for maritime rights; (4) an end to the Near Eastern arms race; and (5) respect for the political independence and territorial integrity of all states of the area.[28] In connection with the fifth point, the President said that there must be adequate recognition of the special interest of three great religions in the Holy Places of Jerusalem. In enumerating these five principles, the President made it clear that they were to be taken together. He said: "We believe there must be progress toward all of them if there is to be progress toward any."[29]

The Security Council considered the matter until June 14, but it was unable to resolve the impasse between those calling for prior Israeli withdrawal and those calling for Israeli withdrawal as part of a larger settlement. The matter passed to the General Assembly on June 17,[30] but it too was unable to resolve the impasse and the question was returned to the Security Council. Finally, on November 22, the Security Council passed a resolution providing guidelines for a just and lasting peace in which Israeli troops would be withdrawn from territories occupied during the conflict, all claims or states of belligerency would be terminated, and the sovereignty, territorial integrity, and political independence of every state in the area and its right to live in peace within secure and recognized boundaries free from threats or acts of force would be acknowledged. The resolution called on the Secretary General to appoint a representative to help the parties reach a settlement along these lines.[31]

The Reunification Measures

In the meantime, Israelis were surprised and jubilant to find East Jerusalem in their hands. Israeli troops prayed at the Wailing Wall on June 7 for the first time in nineteen years. Sentiment swelled for incorporating East Jerusalem into Israel. At first, the Israeli Cabinet was reluctant to take any formal action on Jerusalem while the U.N. was attempting to find a solution to the crisis. Nevertheless, demolition of the barriers separating West and East Jerusalem proceeded apace. Municipal services such as electricity and the telephone system were unified; chronically water-short East Jerusalem was connected to the plentiful West Jerusalem water supply. On June 18, the day after the Arab-Israel crisis moved to the U.N. General Assembly in special session, hundreds of Arabs were evicted from the former Jewish quarter, where they had settled after the Palestine war of 1948. Others were expelled from the Maghribi quarter and an area in front of the Wailing Wall was cleared to create a plaza large enough to accommodate numerous pilgrims who wished to pray at the Wall.[32] A census was conducted in East Jerusalem on June 26.

Then, on June 27, the Knesset passed three laws. The first amended the Law and Administration Ordinance and provided that the law, jurisdiction, and administration of Israel should apply in any area of Eretz Israel* designated by the Government by order.[33] The second was an amendment to

---

*Eretz Israel, or Land of Israel, is used to refer to Israel within its historic boundaries. There is no general agreement among scholars as to exactly where those boundaries lay in ancient times, however, and the Israeli Government has not committed itself on the subject. During the mandate, the term was used in Hebrew by the authorities to designate Palestine. See Great Britain, *Palestine Royal Commission, Memoranda Prepared by the Government of Palestine*, pp. 158-59.

103

the Municipal Corporations Ordinance of 1934 to permit the Minister of Interior to enlarge by proclamation the area of a municipal corporation to include any area designated under the Law and Administration Ordinance.[34] The third measure provided for the protection of the Holy Places and for freedom of access to them.[35] The following day, the Minister of Interior acted to designate under the amended Law and Administration Ordinance the former Jordanian sector of Jerusalem and adjacent territory, including the airport between Qalandiya and Atarot.* He then extended the city limits of Israeli Jerusalem to include these areas.[36]

The reaction to the Israeli action was varied. In Jerusalem itself, the initial reaction was not unfavorable.[37] The populations of East Jerusalem and West Jerusalem mingled freely for the first time in nineteen years. Old acquaintances were renewed; Arabs visited homes they had abandoned two decades previously; and Mayor Teddy Kollek attended the noon prayer services at the Haram al-Sharif on Friday, June 30. In the Arab capitals, however, the reaction was one of anger. Crowds demonstrated in Amman and preachers in the Mosques in Cairo called for a "holy war" to recapture Jerusalem. In a more conciliatory vein, the Secretary General of the World Muslim Congress, Inamullah Khan, talked of functional internationalization of the Holy Places under U.N. control, and he warned that the world's 700 million Muslims would "never accept physical control of their holy places in Jerusalem" by Israel.[38] The U.S. Department of State, with President Johnson's approval, called the Israeli action hasty and said that it could not be "regarded as determining the future of the Holy Places or the future of Jerusalem in relation to them."[39]

In the U.N., the reaction was critical of the Israeli action, but Israeli Foreign Minister Abba Eban in the General Assembly on June 29 described Israel's action as administrative rather than political. He refused to say that East Jerusalem had been annexed and said instead that Jerusalem had been administratively reunified. Nevertheless, the General Assembly passed a Pakistani-sponsored resolution on July 4 refusing to recognize Israel's reunification measures and calling upon

*The airport is now generally referred to as being in Atarot, rather than at Qalandiya as it was previously referred to.

it to rescind them.[40] The U.S. maintained that, semantically, it made no sense for the U.N. to call upon Israel to rescind something which the U.N. did not recognize. Consequently, the U.S. abstained in the voting on the resolution, but it made an official demarche to Israel on the matter. As was to be expected, Israel rejected the U.N. resolution. In a letter to the Secretary General, Foreign Minister Eban said that reunification of the city was a desirable thing and that the Israeli Government was confident that world opinion would welcome the new prospect of seeing Jerusalem "thrive in unity, peace, and spirtual elevation."[41]

These sentiments were echoed in the U.S. by a number of prominent Christian leaders and scholars including Frank M. Cross, Jr., William D. Davies, A. Roy Eckardt, Frederick C. Grant, Reinhold Niebuhr, and James M. Robinson. They said that they saw no justification in "proposals which seek once again to destroy the unity which has been restored to Jerusalem."[42] They noted that during the past twenty years access to the Holy Places had been denied for all Jews and for Israeli Muslims and severely limited for Israeli Christians. They expressed their confidence that free access to the Holy Places would be guaranteed for all by Israel. On the other hand, the National Council of Churches, through the executive committee of its policy-making board, declared on July 14 that it could not approve Israel's annexation of East Jerusalem. The Council urged an international presence to "preserve the peace and integrity of the city, foster the welfare of its inhabitants, and protect its holy shrines with full rights of access to all."[43] The World Council of Churches, meeting in Crete in August, did not go quite so far. It adopted a resolution calling simply for an international agreement guaranteeing access to the Holy Places.[44] Individual Christian bodies in the U.S. generally ignored both the question of Jerusalem and the question of the Holy Places. A Harris poll indicated that some 70 per cent of Americans thought in early July that Jerusalem should be an international city open to all, but by September American opinion had shifted and another Harris poll showed that 43 per cent now thought Israel should be allowed to retain control of the reunified Holy City while only 33 per cent favored internationalization.[45]

Vatican objectives appeared to be more limited in 1967 than they were in 1947 and 1918. The partition of Jerusalem over nineteen years and the relative decline of Christian population in both Israel and Jordan had rendered unrealizable any scheme of erecting a *corpus separatum* with a Christian population large enough to wield significant power. Besides, such an arrangement was not really necessary for perceptible progress toward Christian unity, since *aggiornamento* and the contagion of the ecumenical movement, previously confined largely to Protestant circles, had opened new avenues. In addition, the Vatican was reasonably satisfied with the treatment the Christian shrines had been accorded in Israel.

In a secret consistory on June 26, Pope Paul VI reiterated the Vatican's call for internationalization of Jerusalem.[46] Then, a series of contacts, initiated by Israel, took place during the first ten days of July between the Vatican and the Israeli authorities with a view to finding a formula for handling the problem of the Holy Places in a unified Jerusalem under Israeli control. On July 11, it was reported that the Vatican had dropped its long-standing call for the internationalization of Jerusalem and was studying several Israeli proposals, including the possibility of granting the Holy Places the forms of immunity and inviolability usually accorded embassies and affording the present occupants of the Holy Places the right to administer the shrines without interference from the civil authorities.[47] It is believed that these proposals were discussed with the Oecumenical Patriarch Athenagoras during a visit of the Pope to Turkey on July 25-26.[48] However, the Oecumenical Patriarch is only the first among equals with the other Orthodox prelates and cannot presume to speak authoritatively for the Patriarch of Jerusalem, who, although in communion with the Oecumenical Patriarch, is nevertheless independent.

If the Vatican was negotiating with Israel a satisfactory formula for the Holy Places, it apparently had not made much impression on the Roman Catholic countries in the U.N. On July 14, the General Assembly passed another Pakistani-sponsored resolution, reiterating its call to Israel to rescind all measures already taken and to desist forthwith from any action which would alter the status of Jerusalem.[49] The Roman

Catholic countries supported it, as did the U.K.* The U.S. abstained, reportedly at the direction of President Johnson.[50] The U.S. delegate, Mr. Goldberg, explained that although the U.S. did not recognize any unilateral Israeli action as altering the status of Jerusalem, the U.S. did not believe that a durable peace could be achieved by resolutions dealing with only one aspect of the problem. In the U.S. view, the question of Jerusalem was bound up with the problem of a comprehensive Arab-Israel settlement. While not condemning the U.S. stand in the U.N., the Republican Coordinating Committee took a functional, rather than a territorial, approach and proposed in a statement approved on July 31 that a form of international supervision for the Holy Places be devised.[51] President De Gaulle, in a press conference on November 27, reaffirmed France's position that Jerusalem should be internationalized.[52] As was to be expected, Israel took no action to comply with the U.N. General Assembly resolution. On the other hand, it acceded in late July to the request by the Secretary General that the U.N. be permitted to resume its use of Government House, despite considerable pressure in Israel to make it the official residence of the President of the state.[53]

The reunification measures eventually produced friction within Jerusalem itself. The Ministry for Religious Affairs assumed its responsibilities in East Jerusalem with a heavy hand, even requiring Muslim preachers to submit texts of their Friday sermons for censorship. The result was a meeting on July 24 of twenty-five of Jerusalem's Muslim notables, religious and lay, who subsequently informed the Ministry for Religious Affairs that they did not recognize the unification measures and would not cooperate with the Ministry. The following day, leaflets circulated through East Jerusalem warn-

*Accusing the U.S. and the U.K. of assisting Israel in the war, a number of Arab countries broke diplomatic relations with the U.S. and the U.K. on June 6-7, 1967, and the Arab oil-producing states placed an embargo on oil shipments to the U.S., the U.K., and West Germany. The U.K. was economically hard hit and Foreign Secretary Brown was frequently accused by Israel and its sympathizers in the British Parliament of trying to appease the Arabs on the Jerusalem question and other issues in the hopes of relieving the economic pressure. See *The New York Times*, October 16, 1967, and October 23, 1967; *The Washington Post*, June 27, 1967, and October 18, 1967; and *The Evening Star*, February 19, 1968.

ing against collaboration with the Israeli authorities. The members of the former Municipal Council of East Jerusalem served notice on July 25 that they would not take their seats in the unified Municipal Council. The Israeli Government replied by banishing four of the twenty-five notables from Jerusalem to various parts of Israel for three months and freezing the plan to seat the East Jerusalemites in the unified Municipal Council. Then, as a conciliatory gesture, it removed supervision of Muslim religious affairs from the Ministry for Religious Affairs and placed it in the hands of the Ministry of Defense. The Ministry of Defense promptly cancelled the requirement that sermons be submitted for censorship.[54]

Several days later, a general strike was called for August 7 in a mimeographed leaflet signed by the "Committee for the Defense of Arab Jerusalem." The cause of the strike was probably economic as much as political, reflecting the unhappiness of the merchants with the higher Israeli tax structure and the imposition of customs duties on their inventories.[55] Encouraged by the Jordanian radio, the strike was successful, halting all business activity, including shops and restaurants. The following day, the authorities padlocked the shops of four strike leaders, issued warrants for the arrest of five as organizers, and lifted the license of one of the Arab bus companies for participating in the strike. The Minister for Religious Affairs, Zerah Wahrhaftig, aroused Arab protests again when on August 17 he stated that he considered the Haram al-Sharif Jewish property on the grounds that David had purchased the site from Araunah the Jebusite for fifty shekels of silver.[56] Momentary resistance was also encountered in September when the schools in East Jerusalem were opened with the curriculum used in Arab schools in Israel. Many teachers refused at first to teach in these circumstances but later decided to return to work after they were replaced by Israeli Arabs.

By the fall of 1967, life in Jerusalem seemed to be running fairly smoothly and organized resistance appeared, at least for the moment, to have been broken. In any event, Israel made it clear that the reunification measures were irreversible. Swiss Ambassador Ernesto A. Thalman, appointed in August 1967 by the U.N. Secretary General to report on the situation in Jerusalem, was informed by the Israeli authorities in an unequivocal manner that the process of integration was irreversible and not negotiable.[57] President Shazar told an International Conference of Jewish Journalists on February 15, 1968, that East Jerusalem would remain in Israel's hands and that nothing could compel Israel to withdraw from it. Meanwhile, measures were taken to unify the city demographically as well as administratively. Plans were announced on January 9, 1968, for restoration of the Jewish quarter in the Walled City, and on January 11 some 838 acres of land in the northeast section of East Jerusalem was expropriated for new housing.[58] The expropriation was made under a British mandatory act of 1943 and in accordance with a comprehensive municipal plan drawn up during the mandate by the Town Planning Advisor Henry Kendall and revised slightly by the Israeli authorities after the reunification of the city. Fourteen hundred housing units were planned, some one thousand to be occupied by Jews and four hundred by Arabs. Thus, Israel let it be known by actions as well as by words that they had every intention of keeping East Jerusalem in any settlement.

Chapter 7

Prospects for Settlement

We have traced attempts to solve the Jerusalem question over the past fifty years. Unitl 1936, it was largely a European question, but from that time on it has been an Arab-Jewish problem as well. In fact, at present, it appears that the Arab-Jewish aspect is the more prominent aspect of the problem. But the Europeans, and indeed people around the whole world, still have an interest in how it is settled. President Johnson said on June 19, 1967, that in any settlement of the Jerusalem question, there must be adequate recognition of the special interests of the three great religions in the Holy Places of Jerusalem. Perhaps the best way to examine the kind of settlement necessary is to look at the minimum and maximum positions of those who have an interest in the question.

The Christian Interest

Jerusalem contains a number of shrines which stand on sites celebrated by tradition as the scenes of certain dramatic events connect with Jesus and the early Church. The most important of these are the Church of the Holy Sepulchre in Jerusalem itself and the Church of the Nativity in Bethlehem, not far from Jerusalem. The main interest of Christians has been to assure access to these shrines. The danger faced by pilgrims to the Holy City after its capture by the Seljuks in 1071 helped to spark the Crusades, eventually bringing Christian rule to Jerusalem. With the loss of Jerusalem in 1244, however, Christians were content to settle for the right of access to the city and the shrines. This remains the minimum demand today by all Christians. While Protestants do not have the same attachment to the Church the Holy Sepulchre and the Church of the Nativity as the members of the other branches of Christianity, they nevertheless hold a deep affection for Jerusalem and Bethlehem, both of which have figured prominently in their childhood Sunday school lessons and their adult Bible reading.

In addition, the Roman Catholics, the Orthodox,* and the Armenians have acquired in the course of centuries certain rights in the various shrines, but many of these rights claimed by one group are contested by one or both of the other two groups. As we have seen, each group is less afraid that the ruling authorities might usurp its rights than it is that the ruling authorities will support at its expense one of the other groups having a rival claim. Thus, each of these groups desires the establishment of a regime that will favor it or at least protect it against the other two. The situation was handled during the days of the Ottoman Empire by having outside protectors. The policy of the British was to preserve the status quo, and the international regime envisaged under the U.N. General Assembly resolution of November 29, 1947, was also supposed to maintain the status quo. It would appear therefore that this would also be a minimum requirement by the adherents of these three branches of Christianity, at least until such time as the ecumenical movement produces enough Christian unity to allow the disputes to be settled amicably.

Several possibilities of amicable settlement in the Church of the Holy Sepulchre, for example, come to mind. Of course, complete Christian reunion would bring the most satisfying settlement, but this is unlikely in the near future. Perhaps the three claimants might in time reach agreement themselves on the appointment of the Holy Places Commission envisaged by Article 14 of the mandate instrument but blocked by the ambitions of the European powers. Or perhaps a modified version of a Vatican plan of 1950 for reconstruction of the Church of the Holy Sepulchre might provide an opportunity for a reasonable accommodation. The present structure has been rebuilt several times, the last comprehensive reconstruction having taken place in 1810. Further, it is not of any outstanding beauty. The 1950 Vatican plan called for the erection of a new basilica in the form of a cross, with the tomb occupying a rotunda at the center of the cross.[1] The rotunda would be left open, and a garden would be planted around the tomb. The three arms of the cross would form separate

---

*Meaning here the Orthodox Patriarchate of Jerusalem.

churches for each of the three branches of Christianity now predominating in the present structure. Unfortunately, the Vatican's plan assigned the center and largest arm of the cross to the Latins. However, if this plan were modified to provide for a basilica in the shape of a cross with *four equal-sized* arms, then the three groups in the present church could have equal facilities and the fourth arm would provide a church for the Protestants and other branches of Christianity desiring to be represented in the basilica. Whatever the means of settlement, it must be borne in mind that the problem of the Christian Holy Places is a purely religious one arising out of internal Christian disputes and the essential requirement is to find a way to maintain order without outside interference in the disputes themselves.

The third Christian problem connected with the Jerusalem question is that of the internal politics of the various Christian groups within Jerusalem, notably the Armenian Orthodox and the group adhering to the Orthodox Patriarch of Jerusalem. In neither group does the laity have much say about what goes on, and both Patriarchates are strongly desirous of keeping it that way. This has been the import of most of their testimony to every investigating body charged with recommending a solution to the Jerusalem question from 1936 until the present, and they have been careful to suggest the inclusion of provisions designed to preserve the present state of affairs. In the case of the Orthodox Patriarchate, suggested provisions against interference in internal affairs are meant by the Patriarchate to prevent the Arabizers from getting a foothold in what amounts to a closed Hellenic corporation. In the case of the Armenians, there is no ethnic conflict and the Brotherhood of St. James is only interested in preventing outsiders from having a say in the selection of the Patriarch. While there should be the normal guarantee of religious liberty in Jerusalem, it is highly questionable whether there should be safeguards, especially international safeguards, that would guarantee the perpetuation of a situation in which the laity has little or no say in the management of the affairs of a religious community, particularly where a small foreign ethnic group has captured control of the machinery of the community.

The interest of the European powers in establishing a political arrangement to further their own ambitions of prestige and influence are not part of the general Christian interest. It does not serve the interest of an American Christian, for example, for France or Italy or Greece to pursue a Christian policy in the Near East. It should be evident to everyone that such a policy cannot be successful in a period of intense nationalism such as exists in the area today. Indeed, the Christian population of the Holy Land, both in Israel and Jordan, is declining in relative strength, and the idea of erecting a Christian enclave in this area, such as France has long dreamed of doing, can only end in failure in the circumstances prevailing in the second half of the twentieth century.

To sum up, the basic Christian requirements in a settlement of the Jerusalem question are religious liberty, access to the city of Jerusalem (not just the Holy Places), and provision for the perservation of the status quo in the Christian Holy Places except insofar as the Christian groups themselves freely choose to alter it.

The Muslim Interest

The major Muslim interest in Jerusalem centers around the Haram al-Sharif. With its two mosques, the Dome of the Rock and al-Aqsa Mosque, the Haram al-Sharif covers the spot where Muhammad is believed to have been transported on his Night Journey. In fact, the rock over which the Dome of the Rock is built bears a mark which Islamic tradition says is a footprint left by the Prophet as he ascended into heaven that night.* But the Haram al-Sharif also covers the spot where King Solomon's Temple stood, and for this reason, the Muslims have often feared that if the Jews gained control of Jerusalem, they would tear down the Dome and rebuild the Temple. This argument was advanced by the Muslims in 1929 to support their contention that the Jews should not be allowed to pray at the Wailing Wall, since this might give them a proprietary claim to the Haram al-Sharif.[2] The fear was also expressed to the Royal Commission in 1937 and on other occasions since. No doubt, the statement on August 17, 1967,

---

*Qur'an, XVII, 1. It was also upon this rock that tradition says Abraham offered to sacrifice Isaac. Genesis XXII: 1-14.

by Israeli Minister of Religious Affairs Zerah Wahrhaftig that the Haram al-Sharif was Jewish property only served to confirm Muslim fears that the Dome would soon be destroyed and work begun on the reconstruction of the Temple. It would therefore seem that one essential ingredient for any settlement of the Jerusalem question would have to be a guarantee that the Haram al-Sharif will not be taken from the Muslims.

Access to the Haram al-Sharif would also appear to be an essential Muslim requirement in any settlement of the Jerusalem question. The U.N. General Assembly resolution of December 11, 1948, required only that the Holy Places be made accessible to all the inhabitants of Palestine.[3] In the case of the Haram al-Sharif, this resolution is now being complied with for the first time in twenty years. But wider access than this is required if a real settlement is to be brought about. According to the best available information, there are probably between 400 and 500 million Muslims in the world. Since approximately 100 million of these are Arabs, only 300 to 400 million or 75 to 80 per cent of the world's Muslims have access to the Muslim Holy Places in Jerusalem in the present circumstances. Presumably, any settlement would provide for free access for all Muslims.

It is often asserted that Muslims insist that Jerusalem, or at least the Walled City containing the Muslim Holy Places, must be in Muslim hands. This contention will not bear the scrutiny of history. Sultan al-Kamil, the nephew of Salah al-Din, offered in 1219 to exchange Jerusalem for Damietta, which had been captured by the Fifth Crusade; and in 1229 al-Kamil negotiated with Frederick II a treaty under which Nazareth, Bethlehem, and Jerusalem were ceded to Frederick in exchange for Frederick's aid against al-Kamil's enemies.* Although the Arab League states called in 1947 for an Arab Jerusalem in an Arab Palestine, they changed their tune after Jerusalem was partitioned between Israel and Jordan and called for internationalization, preferring this solution to the continuation of the Walled City in Jordanian hands. Their present call for a return of the Walled City to Jordan stems

*Frederick II had married Isabelle of Brienne, the heir to the throne of Jerusalem. He was crowned King of Jerusalem in the Church of the Holy Sepulchre on March 18, 1229. Carl Brockelmann, *History of the Islamic Peoples*, p. 232; and Philip K. Hitti, *History of the Arabs*, p. 654.

more from a desire to keep it out of Israeli hands than from a heartfelt desire to see it once more in Jordanian hands. The same is true of the stand of the other Muslim states, such as Pakistan, which supported the U.N. General Assembly resolutions of July 4 and July 14, 1967.

In support of the Muslim claim to Jerusalem, it is sometimes claimed that Jerusalem was predominantly a Muslim city prior to 1948. There does not appear to be any evidence that Muslims ever constituted a majority in Jerusalem, except possibly sometime during the period from the mid-thirteenth century until the beginning of the nineteenth century. One authority says that until the time of the Crusades, the majority of the population was Christian and Jewish, rather than Muslim.[4] Christians were presumably the major element during the period of the Latin kingdom. In 1668, however, Muslims were estimated to constitute 74.5 per cent of the population; but by 1838, the Muslim element had declined to 40.9 per cent of that total.[5] Another authority estimates that in 1873 Muslims constituted roughly 37 per cent of the population, but reports from the American Consulate in Jerusalem indicated that Muslims have not exceeded 25 per cent of the population over the past one hundred years.[6] Even within the Walled City, the census of 1931 showed the Muslim population to be only 48.4 per cent of the total, and in 1946 it was still estimated to be only 48 per cent of the total.[7]

The desire of King Husayn to regain control of East Jerusalem is based primarily on economic and nationalistic considerations. The Walled City is a great tourist attraction and constituted for Jordan the most important source of foreign exchange during the nineteen years it was under Jordanian control. Not only did tourists come to see the shrines and spend money in the souvenir shops in the Walled City, but since Jerusalem was centrally located for travel to other nearby spots of interest, many tourists stayed in the modern hotels of East Jerusalem outside the walls while they took side trips to Bethlehem, Hebron, and the towns of Samaria. Thus, the loss of the Walled City has meant a serious loss of hard currency for Jordan.

But the economic considerations must not be overplayed. Jordan was able to monopolize the tourist trade in the Walled City only because of the legal state of war that existed between

Jordan and Israel. Jordan would permit only one-way crossings at the Mandelbaum Gate, thus preventing tourists from staying in West Jerusalem hotels and crossing to East Jerusalem only for the day. Under conditions of peace, Jordan would not have the same advantage even if the Walled City were returned. Assuming a peaceful border which may be crossed freely, the Walled City would be as accessible from West Jerusalem as from East Jerusalem. Bethlehem, a suburb of Jerusalem, is more accessible under peaceful conditions from West Jerusalem than from East Jerusalem. In these circumstances, money spent in the Walled City would benefit Jordan, but East Jerusalem hotels would have to compete with West Jerusalem hotels. Even if the Walled City were not returned, Jordan would be able under conditions of peace to benefit somewhat from the tourist trade provided Bethlehem is returned to Jordan. Bethlehem is an attraction in itself for the Chrisitan tourist trade. If a number of modern hotels were constructed there, tourists could cross into Jerusalem for the day as easily as they could cross the other way.

Probably the most important consideration for Jordan is the nationalist aspiration of both East Bank and West Bank Jordanians for the recovery of the Walled City. On the whole, Jordanians have preferred to live near the seat of government rather than in Jerusalem, and for that reason, population and industry have gravitated to Amman, which grew from a small town of 30,000 in 1947 to 311,134 by 1967. But even though Amman has come to be the Jordanian metropolis, it does not offer the same prestige as the city with the third most sacred shrine in Islam. In addition, the fear of Muslims everywhere that the Dome of the Rock and al-Aqsa Mosque may be replaced by a reconstructed Jewish Temple adds to the nationalist pressure on Jordan to seek the recovery of East Jerusalem. Indeed, Jerusalem appears to be the most formidable question with which King Husayn must deal in arriving at a settlement with Israel. Since it is a symbol of Palestine and the Palestine problem, any settlement that would leave the Walled City in Israeli hands must appear to Arabs everywhere as a sell-out on the Palestine cause itself. In these circumstances, Husayn would find it risky to go to the negotiating table with the Israelis unless he had the other Arabs with him or unless he had prior assurances of a reasonable concession on Jerusalem.

116

To sum up, the most important considerations for the Muslim world are free access to the Muslim shrines in Jerusalem and a guarantee that the Dome of the Rock and al-Aqsa Mosque will remain Muslim shrines controlled by Muslims. Economic considerations are also of some importance for Jordan, but in any peaceful settlement, Jordan will never be able to monopolize the tourist trade as it did before June 1967. Even more important for Jordan than economic considerations are nationalist aspirations to recover the Walled City.

The Jewish Interest

The Jewish interest in Jerusalem is both religious and nationalistic. The Hebrew people have been connected with Jerusalem since its capture by David about 1000 B.C., and with the birth of Judaism during the Babylonian captivity (587-39 B.C.), Jerusalem became the center of Jewish longing. The Prophets foretold the return to Zion, and the Psalmist vowed never to forget the City of David:

> If I forget thee, O Jerusalem,
>   let my right hand forget her cunning.
> If I do not remember thee,
>   let my tongue cleave to the roof
>   of my mouth;
>   if I prefer not Jerusalem above
>   my chief joy.
>
> (Psalms CXXXVII: 5-6)

When the Romans destroyed the Second Temple in A.D. 70 and exiled the Jews in A.D. 135, this same sentiment dominated the Jewish spirit. The Jew longed for the return to Jerusalem, the reestablishment of Israel, and the rebuilding of the Temple. The Jewish prayer book was (and still is) replete with references to Jerusalem (or Zion) as the object of Jewish yearning. Salvation was thought of as an earthly restoration of the Kingdom of Israel through the work of a Messiah. Individual salvation had meaning for the Jew only in the sense that he was destined to live again in the restored Kingdom.

In time, Jerusalem became for many Jews a symbol denoting the Heavenly City, rather than a geographical location, just as Israel came to mean simply the people of God. Nevertheless, Jews continued to be attracted to the earthly city and except for the period of the Crusades, there seem to have always been Jews, though not always in large numbers, in Jerusalem from the time of Constantine to the present. It was not until the second half of the nineteenth century, however, that they became once again the majority of the inhabitants. In 1837, an earthquake caused severe damage in Safad, one of the main centers of Jewish life in Palestine at the time. Some 3,000 of the Safad Jews moved south to Jerusalem, greatly increasing the small Jewish community there. But the real Jewish influx began with the founding of the new city outside the walls in 1860 by Sir Moses Montefiore. In 1869, the American Consul in Jerusalem reported that Jews already constituted half the population of Jerusalem.

With the rapid growth of the Zionist movement after the First Zionist Congress in 1897, Zion (or Jerusalem) and Israel resumed their full geographical meaning and took on a political or nationalistic connotation as well. Jerusalem came once again to be regarded as the capital of the Jewish people, even by those who did not favor the creation of a Jewish state. Those who favored a Jewish state found it difficult to envisage a Jewish state without at least the modern Jewish sections of the city being part of it, and every plan put forth by the Jewish Agency, with the exception of the 1946 plan, called for the inclusion of these areas of the city in the Jewish state. The sentiment of the Jewish nationalist was summed up in Hatikva, the anthem of the Zionist movement and later the national anthem of Israel:

> ...We have not lost our hope,
> the hope of two thousand years,
> to be a free people in our own land,
> in the land of Zion and in Jerusalem.

If the Jewish Agency was willing in 1947 to agree to internationalization of the whole city of Jerusalem under the U.N. partition plan, it was only because it believed that this was the short-term price that would have to be paid for the creation of a Jewish state, and that in the long term the whole of Jerusalem would be included in Israel when the international regime came up for review at the end of the first decade. But the U.N. was unable to put its plan into effect and it was unable to protect Jerusalem from the ordeal of war in 1948. Bernadotte's proposal in June 1948 that all of Jerusalem be turned over to King Abdallah only served to harden Jewish feeling that since they had managed to hold on to West Jerusalem during the war, they should hold on to it in peace.

If there was strong feeling in 1948 that Israel should hold on to that part of Jerusalem won by Jewish blood, the feeling is even stronger today in regard to the whole city. The Jordanian period was one of the few periods in history when Jews were not allowed to pray at the Wailing Wall. Even during the period of the Roman Emperor Hadrian, when Jews were not allowed to reside in Jerusalem, they were allowed on the feast of the Ninth of Av (Tisha b'Av) to pray at the Wailing Wall to commemorate the destruction of the Temple. Neither the U.N. nor any of the great powers were willing to force Jordan to grant access to the Wailing Wall. Having acquired free access to the Wailing Wall in 1967, it is doubtful that any Jew would now think seriously of returning it to Jordanian hands. Similarly, it is doubtful that any nationalist-minded Israeli would consider redividing the city and returning the Walled City to Jordan. For the Israeli nationalist, the reunification of the City under Israeli rule represents a worthy achievement of the Jewish people fulfilling collectively the role of the Messiah.

To sum up, free access to the Wailing Wall is an important interest of all Jews, and it is doubtful that any arrangement that compromises this interest would be acceptable. For the nationalist-minded Israeli, the idea of giving up the center of the national life of the state would probably also be unthinkable.

Devices for Solution

Now that we have considered the interests and requirements of the various groups interested in Jerusalem, we should look at some of the solutions frequently put forward and see how useful they could be in reconciling the interests of the various parties.

Condominium. The Arab and the communist states (except Romania) have been calling for a return to the status quo before June 5, 1967. Presumably, this would mean the return of East Jerusalem to Jordanian hands. This, of course, would solve the problem of guarantees for the Haram al-Sharif. It would also appeal to Jordan's nationalist aspirations, and it would allow Jordan to make other concessions likely to bring about a peace settlement with Israel. As already pointed out, it would not restore Jordan's monopoly of the tourist trade and all the financial benefits accruing from it. Further, Israel would not agree to this plan, since it would mean redivision of the city and return of the Wailing Wall and the Jewish cemetery on the Mount of Olives to Jordanian hands.

One of the time-honored devices for dealing with an area which two nations desire is a condominium. Israel would, of course, oppose a condominium over the whole city, since it would mean sharing sovereignty with another state or other states over its capital. This device could therefore be considered only for the Walled City. The natural choices for the powers to exercise the condominium are Jordan and Israel. Such an arrangement would of course help satisfy Jordanian nationalist feeling and solve the problem of the Muslim and Jewish Holy Places. On the other hand, the Christians might well raise the question as to who is going to represent them in the condominium. Greece would probably seem to the Orthodox Patriarchate as the logical choice for this role; Lebanon would probably be favored by the Uniats; France, Italy, Spain, or Austria would probably suit the Latins best; and Great Britain or a Scandinavian country might be favored by the Protestants.

In any event, the condominium device is clumsy and presents a number of problems, such as the selection of the executive to head the local government and the personal loyalties of the officials and civil servants. Even if it was agreed that both Israeli and Jordanian currencies could circulate, there would be the problem of two different customs procedures. There would also be the problem of two legal systems and the problem of which state's supreme court would decide appeals from the Jerusalem courts. In short, the condominium device was invented for a period in history when government and national feeling were not so all-embracing as they are today.

Territorial Internationalization. The territorial internationalization device is simpler than the condominium. However, this solution died during the last half of May 1948, since neither Jordan nor Israel was willing to implement it in the changed circumstances. If this plan could be revived now, it would, of course, solve the problem of access to the Holy Places for all of the various religious groups. It would not, however, automatically solve the problem connected with the internal affairs of the Orthodox Patriarchate, since the struggle between the Arabizers and the Hellenizers would go on and would plague the city's administrators until the Arabizers won, unless special provisions against lay interference in the Patriarchate's affairs were included in the city's statute. Internationalization would guarantee that the Haram al-Sharif would not be taken out of Muslim hands, but it would not solve the problem of Jordan's diminished national prestige resulting from the loss of the walled portion of Islam's third holiest city. It would mean a tremendous financial loss to Israel, since its second largest city would be severed from the country. Further, it is unlikely that Israel would willingly give up the center of its national life, and thus the plan becomes impractical. As the U.S. Representative to the Trusteeship Council is reported to have said in 1949, no plan for Jerusalem is practical that requires the use of American troops to implement it.[8] If the U.N. could not or would not implement such a plan in 1949, it will certainly not be able to do so now. Even if Israel were willingly to agree to internationalization on the basis of the 1947 plan, the city is even more overwhelmingly Jewish in 1968 than it was in 1947.* If a referendum were taken at the end of the first decade, Jerusalem would opt for union with Israel.

Perhaps Israel could be persuaded to agree to territorial internationalization of the Walled City. Even this is problematical, since it means redivision of the city, something to which not only nationalist-minded Israelis but a great many other people who do not like the idea of divided cities would be opposed. On the other hand, Foreign Minister Sharett proposed this solution in 1949 and 1950. In any event, many

*In 1967, 73 per cent of the population was Jewish, as compared with 60 per cent in 1947. See Appendix A.

of the same comments would apply to this suggestion as apply to the suggestion that the whole city be internationalized. It would solve the problem of access to the Holy Places for all of the various religious groups. It would not solve the internal problems of the Orthodox Patriarchate. It would furnish a safeguard for the Haram al-Sharif, but it would not restore to Jordan the prestige of controlling the Walled City. It would in no way restore Jordan's monopoly of the tourist trade. It might alleviate Jordan's financial loss if the internationalized Walled City were in a customs and monetary union with Jordan, but Israel is unlikely to agree to this, since it would look too much like returning the Walled City to Jordan. A customs-free zone in the Walled City would present difficulties for both Israel and Jordan, and the Israelis would probably insist that the Walled City be in a customs and monetary union with Israel.

A U.N. Trust. A variation on the theme of territorial internationalization is the idea of transforming Jerusalem into a U.N. trust, with Israel as the permanent trustee. Israel is unlikely to agree to this, since it would mean that the capital of the country would not be on its own territory but on that of the U.N. trust. On the other hand, it might agree to making the Walled City into such a trust. This would permit a unified administration for the whole city, with the Walled City constituting perhaps a borough within the larger unit. Those residents who wished could become Israeli citizens and the others would be Israeli subjects, but both would have the same rights and privileges before the law. Complaints of unequal treatment could be brought to the attention of the U.N. Trusteeship Council. Guarantees of the status quo in the Holy Places, as well as of free access to them, could be written into the trust instrument, thereby allowing appeal to the Trusteeship Council in the case of complaints or violations. Christian, Muslim, and Jewish religious interests would be protected under such an arrangement, but it would not satisfy Jordanian nationalist aspirations and it would require a sacrifice of some Israeli nationalist feelings.

Outside Protectors. We also need to consider what provisions are necessary to satisfy the other parties if Israel insists on retaining the whole city. The question of the status quo in the Christian Holy Places could be resolved by a form of functional internationalization of the Holy Places under a U.N. commissioner, such as Sweden and the Netherlands proposed in 1949 and 1950. Such an arrangement would also provide the guarantee needed to quell Muslim fears for the safety of the Haram al-Sharif. Another useful device would be to place the various Holy Places under the protection of individual foreign states. One way to do this is for Israel to grant a particular Holy Place the status of an embassy of the protecting state. King Husayn could thus be the protector of Muslim shrines in Jerusalem, and the Haram al-Sharif could enjoy the immunities of a Jordanian embassy. In cases where a Christian shrine is in the hands of one Christian group, the same device could be used. For example, shrines solely in the hands of Latins could be placed under the protection of the Vatican; and Great Britain could be the protector of the Protestant shrine of the Garden Tomb. But this form of the protector system would be more difficult to apply in the case of some of the principal Christian Holy Places, such as the Church of the Holy Sepulchre, where the shrine is divided among various Christian groups. Here it might be better to revive the system as it existed in the nineteenth century. France, or some other Catholic power such as Spain, Italy, or Austria, could assume the role of protector of Latin rights. If the U.S.S.R. does not have the qualifications that Imperial Russia had for the role of protector of Orthodox rights, another Orthodox state could assume this role. If Greece became the Orthodox protector, no doubt the Hellenizing element in the Orthodox Patriarchate would be strengthened. A protector would also have to be found for Armenian rights.

In reviving the protector system, Israel may insist that the protection extended by the protecting powers relate only to the Holy Places and not to the Chrisitian communities in the country. In the case of the Holy Places controlled by more than one group, the role of the protector might be limited to participation in naming an arbitration commission when disputes arise in these Holy Places. Provision might be made, for example, for each protector whose client's rights are disputed to name one commissioner, and for the commissioners thus named to elect another commissioner from outside their number to be chairman of the commission. The decision of the arbitration commission would then be final.

By some such device, the necessary guarantees could be had for freedom of access to and the preservation of the status quo in the Holy Places even if Israel retained the whole city. But neither functional internationalization nor the protector system would requite Jordanian nationalist aspirations to recover the Walled City. A Jordanian flag over the Haram al-Sharif would of course be preferable to a U.N. flag. Perhaps, if Israel would permit Jordanian citizens to reside, work, and own property in Jerusalem and to repatriate their earnings, Jordan could share again in the economic life of the city. Even so, the sacrifice in terms of Jordanian nationalist aspirations would be considerable.

Borough System. Another device sometimes mentioned is the borough system. Under this arrangement, Jerusalem would be a unified city composed of several boroughs. West Jerusalem would be transformed into one or more Jewish boroughs and the portion of East Jerusalem outside the walls would be made into one or more Arab boroughs. The Walled City would be consitituted a separate mixed borough or divided, with the Jewish quarter being incorporated into one of the Jewish boroughs of West Jerusalem and the rest of the area within the walls included in one of the Arab boroughs of East Jerusalem. The unified city would have at its head a mayor responsible for central administrative services, while local matters in each borough would be left in the hands of a borough council and a borough president.

Israel might agree to such a solution, provided the arrangement did not, in effect, result in redivision of the city or a condominium with Jordan. This means that Israel would probably insist that the city be considered part of the Israeli state. Jordan, on the other hand, is unlikely to consider any arrangement that did not provide for an important Jordanian role in the city. If Jordanians were given the right to live, work, and own property in the city and to repatriate their earnings freely, Jordan could share in the economic life of the city. By utilizing the outside protector system, Jordan could be given the role of protector of the Muslim Holy Places. In addition, if the Walled City were constituted a separate borough and Jordan were given some say in its administration, then it would even have a civil role in Jerusalem. This might be done by allowing the Jordanian and Israeli governments to appoint a number of councillors on the borough council or perhaps to name by turns the borough president. Thus, the borough system would assure a large measure of self-government for both the Jews and the Arabs in the city. Satisfactory arrangements could be made for protection of the Holy Places. The sacrifice in Israeli nationalist feelings would not be overwhelming. While Jordanian nationalist aspirations would not be fully satisfied, a substantial role for Jordan in the life of the city could be devised.

The Lesson

It should be clear from this study that the Jerusalem question is not a simple one. In the most restricted sense, the question is essentially an Israeli-Jordanian one, and thus it is between Israel and Jordan that agreement must ultimately be reached on the territorial and political aspects of the problem. On the other hand, no agreement between Jordan and Israel is possible until the larger religious requirements, particularly the Muslim requirements, are met, since even if accommodation is possible on all other issues, Jordan could not afford to flaunt Muslim public opinion, particularly in the other Arab countries, by reaching an agreement with Israel that did not provide for guarantees for the Haram al-Sharif. Likewise, as long as minimum Muslim demands on Jerusalem are not met, the chances of settlement between Israel and the other Arab states appear slim. It is doubtful that any Arab government could afford to risk the public reaction that would follow an agreement with Israel before this question is resolved. Thus, the Jerusalem question could become a stumbling block to any comprehensive Near Eastern settlement.

But it is not just Muslim demands that must be met. Even if Israel and Jordan came to an agreement on Jerusalem, it would not receive the blessing of the world community through the United Nations until the minimum Christian demands are also met. This is the lesson of 1949 and 1950, when the U.N. insisted on territorial internationalization of the whole city despite Israeli and Jordanian opposition.

The purpose of this study has not been to put forth a solution to the Jerusalem question but only to delineate the problem and to point out the major demands that must be satisfied. Not every demand can be met, but the larger ones must certainly be met before choices can be made on the others. This is the lesson of fifty years of the Jerusalem question.

Appendixes

Notes

Bibliography

Index

Appendix A

POPULATION OF JERUSALEM, 1800-1967

	Jews	per cent	Muslims	per cent	Christians	per cent	Others	per cent	Total	per cent
1800	1,000	10.0			3,500	31.8			10,000	100
1838	3,000	27.3	4,500	40.9	3,500	31.8			11,000	100
1873	4,000	26.7	6,000	40.0	5,000	33.3			15,000	100
1884	20,000	50.0	10,000	25.0	10,000	25.0			40,000	100
1887	25,000	50.0	12,500	25.0	12,500	25.0			50,000	100
1898	41,000	67.4	7,000	11.5	12,800	21.1			60,800	100
1905	40,000	66.6	7,000	11.7	13,000	21.7			60,000	100
1912	45,000	64.3	10,000	14.3	15,000	21.4			70,000	100
1922	33,971	54.3	13,413	21.4	14,699	23.5	495	.8	62,578	100
1931	51,222	56.6	19,894	22.0	19,335	21.4	52	.0	90,503	100
1944	97,000	61.7	30,630	19.5	29,350	18.7	100	.1	157,080	100
1946	99,320	60.4	33,680	20.4	31,330	19.1	110	.1	164,440	100
1952 W	138,000	99.3			1,000	.7			139,000	100
1952 E									47,000	100
Total	138,000	74.2							186,000	100

(Continued)

POPULATION OF JERUSALEM, 1800-1967 *(Continued)*

	Jews	per cent	Muslims	per cent	Christians	per cent	Others	per cent	Total	per cent
1961 W	165,022	98.6			2,413	1.4			167,435	100
E			49,504	81.8	10,982	18.2	2	.0	60,488	100
Total	165,022	72.4	49,504	21.7	13,395	5.9	2	.0	227,923	100
1966 W	193,020	98.6			2,680	1.4			195,700	100
E			57,400	82.0	12,600	18.0			70,000	100
Total	193,020	72.6	57,400	21.6	15,280	5.8			265,700	100
1967	194,000	73.3	55,000	20.8	15,500	5.8	300	.1	264,800	100

Sources

1800 James Parkes, *The Story of Jerusalem*, p. 18.
1838 Charles M. Watson, *The Story of Jerusalem*, p. 278. Michael Avi-Yonah, David H. K. Amiran, Julius Jotham Rothschild, and H. M. Z. Meyer, *Jerusalem, The Saga of the Holy City*, p. 40.
1873 Israel P. Warren, *Jerusalem Ancient and Modern*, pp. 46-47.
1884 Frank E. Manuel, *The Realities of American-Palestine Relations*, p. 69.
1887 *Ibid.*
1898 Karl Baedeker, *Palestine and Syria, 1898*, p. 33.
1905 Charles W. Wilson and Charles M. Watson, "Jerusalem," *Encyclopedia Britannica* (11th ed.), XV, 335.
1912 Karl Baedeker, *Palestine and Syria, 1912*, p. 24.
1922 Palestine, *A Survey of Palestine*, Vol. I, p. 148.
1931 *Ibid.*
1944 *Ibid.*, p. 151.
1946 Palestine, *Supplement to Survey of Palestine*, p. 13.
1952 Israel, Central Bureau of Statistics, *Statistical Abstract of Israel*, 1952-53, pp. 10-11; and Paul G. Phillips, *The Hashemite Kingdom: Prolegomena to a Technical Assistance Program*, p. 72.
1961 Israel, Central Bureau of Statistics, *Statistical Abstract of Israel*, 1962, p. 57; and Jordan, Department of Statistics, *First Census of Population and Housing, 18 November, 1961, Interim Report No. 7, Distribution and Characteristics of Population, Jerusalem District*, p. 72.
1966 Israel, Central Bureau of Statistics, *Statistical Abstract of Israel*, 1967, p. 30.
1967 Israel, Census of June 26, 1967, reported in *The New York Times*, October 4, 1967, and United Nations, S/8146, p. 4. Figures for East Jerusalem are estimates; see *The New York Times*, March 20, 1968.

Appendix B

Summary of Plans Discussed in the Text

1. Tripartite (Sykes-Picot) Agreement of 1916 and Agreement of St. Jean de Maurienne of 1917. (Text discussion, p. 3.)

   General Provisions. International administration to be established in Palestine west of the Jordan between Haifa and Gaza.

   Sovereignty over Jerusalem. City included in international zone.

   Protection of Holy Places. Not elaborated.

   Arab Reaction. Agreements regarded as inconsistent with Husayn-McMahon correspondence.

   Jewish Reaction. Regarded as threat to fulfillment of Balfour Declaration.

   Fate of Plan. Superseded by Lloyd George-Clemenceau Agreement of December 1918.

2. Lloyd George-Clemenceau Agreement of December 1918. (Text discussion, pp. 5-6.)

   General Provisions. Great Britain to have control in Palestine.

   Sovereignty over Jerusalem. City under British control.

   Protection of Holy Places. French claimed that agreement had been given on condition that question of Holy Places be resolved to satisfaction of France. British disputed this.

   Arab Reaction. Agreement not made public until after assignment of mandate.

   Jewish Reaction. Agreement not made public until after assignment of mandate.

   Fate of Plan. Embodied in British mandate over Palestine.

3. King-Crane Commission Report of August 28, 1919. (Text discussion, pp. 19-20.)

   General Provisions. Palestine to be included in a united Syrian state. Syria to be under mandate.

   Sovereignty over Jerusalem. Jerusalem to be part of Syria.

   Protection of Holy Places. Holy Places should be cared for by an international and interreligious commission under the oversight and approval of the mandatory and the League of Nations.

Arab Reaction. Report not published until 1922.

Jewish Reaction. Report not published until 1922.

Fate of Plan. Shelved by Allied Powers at Paris Peace Conference.

4. Draft Mandate for Palestine of December 1920. (Text discussion, pp. 5-16.)

General Provisions. Palestine to be placed under British mandate.

Sovereignty over Jerusalem. Jerusalem to be part of British-mandated Palestine.

Protection of Holy Places. Holy Places Commission to be appointed to study and regulate questions and claims.

Arab Reaction. Arabs called for Palestine Arab state.

Jewish Reaction. Accepted mandate.

Fate of Plan. Approved by League Council with minor modifications. Holy Places Commission provision reserved.

5. Royal Commission Plan of July 7, 1937 (Peel Commission). (Text discussion, pp. 23-30.)

General Provisions. Partition of Palestine into Jewish and Arab states and a permanent British mandatory zone. Arab state to be joined to Transjordan.

Sovereignty over Jerusalem. City to be part of permanent British mandatory zone.

Protection of Holy Places. Great Britain to be permanent international trustee.

Arab Reaction. Amir Abdallah of Transjordan favored it. Rest of Arabs called for transformation of Palestine into independent Arab state.

Jewish Reaction. Opinion split. Jewish Agency finally accepted idea of partition but disagreed with Commission report on details of plan. It put forth plan of its own.

Fate of Plan. British Government appointed new Commission to elaborate partition plan.

6. Jewish Agency Plan of 1937. (Text discussion, pp. 28-29.)

General Provisions. Partition of Palestine and Transjordan into Jewish and Arab states and a permanent British mandatory zone.

Sovereignty over Jerusalem. City to be divided between Jewish state and mandatory zone.

Protection of Holy Places. Great Britain to be permanent international trustee.

Arab Reaction. Amir Abdallah of Transjordan favored Peel Commission plan. Rest of Arabs called for transformation of Palestine into independent Arab state.

Jewish Reaction.

Fate of Plan. Rejected by Palestine Partition Commission.

7. Palestine Partition Commission Plan of October 1938 (Woodhead Commission). (Text discussion, pp. 30-32.)

    General Provisions. Three alternative plans presented for partition of Palestine into Jewish and Arab states and mandatory zones. However, report ended with recommendation against all three.

    Sovereignty over Jerusalem. City to be part of mandatory zone in all three partition plans.

    Protection of Holy Places. Great Britain to be permanent international trustee in all three partition plans.

    Arab Reaction. Report recommended against partition. Regarded as advance in recognition of Arab viewpoint.

    Jewish Reaction. Report was regarded as disappointing.

    Fate of Plan. After outlining its three plans in its report, Woodhead Commission recommended against any partition plan.

8. White Paper of May 17, 1939. (Text discussion, pp. 32-33.)

    General Provisions. Palestine to be transformed within 10 years into independent state in treaty relationship with Great Britain.

    Sovereignty over Jerusalem. Jerusalem to be capital of new state.

    Protection of Holy Places. Provisions to be included in Palestinian constitution or in Anglo-Palestinian treaty to assure the security of, and freedom of access to, the Holy Places and the protection of the interests of the various religious bodies.

    Arab Reaction. While it was endorsed by some, most Arabs regarded it as insufficient.

    Jewish Reaction. Regarded as betrayal of national home provision of mandate. Great bitterness over immigration restrictions.

    Fate of Plan. Found to be unworkable by mandatory power.

9. Anglo-American Committee Report of April 22, 1946. (Text discussion, pp. 38-39.)

    General Provisions. Palestine to be placed under long-term trusteeship arrangement leading eventually to independence.

    Sovereignty over Jerusalem. Jerusalem to be capital of Palestine.

    Protection of Holy Places. International guarantees.

    Arab Reaction. Arabs called for immediate transformation of Palestine into independent Arab state.

    Jewish Reaction. Jewish Agency said problem could not be solved without a Jewish state.

    Fate of Plan. Joint Anglo-American technical committee appointed to work out details.

10. Morrison-Grady Plan of July 25, 1945. (Text discussion, pp. 39-40.)

General Provisions. Palestine to be transformed into a cantonal state, composed of an autonomous Jewish province, an autonomous Arab province, and two areas under direct control of the central government.

Sovereignty over Jerusalem. Jerusalem to be under direct control of central government.

Protection of Holy Places. Under protection of British High Commissioner, who would be head of central government.

Arab Reaction. Arabs called for immediate transformation of Palestine into independent Arab state.

Jewish Reaction. Rejected by Jewish Agency, which did not like details of plan, particularly immigration provisions.

Fate of Plan. U.S. refused to support plan.

11. Jewish Agency Plan of 1946. (Text discussion, p. 40.)

General Provisions. Partition of Palestine into Jewish and Arab states.

Sovereignty over Jerusalem. Jerusalem included in Arab state.

Protection of Holy Places. Not elaborated.

Arab Reaction. Arabs called for immediate transformation of Palestine into independent Arab state.

Jewish Reaction. Not applicable.

Fate of Plan. Palestine question referred to U.N.

12. UNSCOP Minority Plan of August 31, 1947. (Text discussion, pp. 43-45.)

General Provisions. Transformation of Palestine within 3 years into independent federal state composed of a Jewish province and an Arab province.

Sovereignty over Jerusalem. Jerusalem to be federal capital.

Protection of Holy Places. Holy Places to be under supervision and protection of a permanent international body.

Arab Reaction. Arabs called for transformation of Palestine into independent Arab state.

Jewish Reaction. Rejected by Jewish Agency, which favored majority plan.

Fate of Plan. Rejected by Ad Hoc Committee of U.N. General Assembly.

13. UNSCOP Majority Plan of August 31, 1947. (Text discussion, pp. 43-47.)

General Provisions. Partition of Palestine into an Arab state, a Jewish state, and an international zone.

Sovereignty over Jerusalem. Jerusalem area to be constituted an international zone administered by the U.N.

Protection of Holy Places. Protected by international trustee.

Arab Reaction. Arabs called for unified independent Arab Palestine.

Jewish Reaction. Plan accepted by Jewish Agency.

Fate of Plan. Accepted by U.N. General Assembly on November 29, 1947, with minor modifications.

14. Bernadotte's Preliminary Proposals of June 1948. (Text discussion, pp. 59-64.)

    General Provisions. Transformation of Palestine and Jordan into union composed of two members, one Jewish and one Arab.

    Sovereignty over Jerusalem. Jerusalem to be included in the Arab member, with municipal autonomy for the Jewish community.

    Protection of Holy Places. Special arrangements for the protection of the Holy Places.

    Arab Reaction. Proposals favored by King Abdallah, but rejected by Arab League, which called for unitary Arab state in Palestine.

    Jewish Reaction. Proposals rejected by Provisional Government of Israel, which did not like immigration provisions or provisions on Jerusalem.

    Fate of Plan. Revised by Bernadotte.

15. Bernadotte's Proposal of September 16, 1948. (Text discussion, pp. 65-68.)

    General Provisions. Partition of Palestine into Arab and Jewish states, with Arab state united with Jordan.

    Sovereignty over Jerusalem. Jerusalem to be placed under U.N. control, but with maximum feasible local autonomy for its Arab and Jewish communities.

    Protection of Holy Places. Safeguards to be provided for protection of Holy Places and free access to them.

    Arab Reaction. Proposal opposed by Arab League, which called for unitary Arab state in Palestine.

    Jewish Reaction. Proposal rejected by Provisional Government of Israel, which did not like territorial provisions.

    Fate of Plan. Shelved by First Committee of U.N. General Assembly.

16. U.N. General Assembly Resolution 194 (III) of December 11, 1948. (Text discussion, p. 68.)

    General Provisions. Establishment of Conciliation Commission to promote Palestine settlement.

    Sovereignty over Jerusalem. Jerusalem to have permanent international regime, with provision for maximum local autonomy for distinctive groups consistent with the special international status.

    Protection of Holy Places. Under U.N. supervision.

    Arab Reaction. Arabs reserved opinion on Jerusalem provision until they could see Commission's proposals.

Jewish Reaction. Israel opposed territorial internationalization of West Jerusalem, but expressed willingness to discuss functional internationalization of Holy Places.

Fate of Plan. Conciliation Commission developed plan for Jerusalem.

17. Palestine Conciliation Commission Plan of Sept. 1, 1949. (Text discussion, pp. 72-78.)

General Provisions. Dealt with Jerusalem.

Sovereignty over Jerusalem. Permanent international regime for Jerusalem. However, city would be divided into two zones, an Arab zone administered by Jordan and a Jewish zone administered by Israel.

Protection of Holy Places. Within competence of the U.N. Commissioner, system of international courts would deal with questions involving Holy Places.

Arab Reaction. Except for Jordan, Arabs called for full territorial internationalization of city. Jordan opposed any form of internationalization for East Jerusalem.

Jewish Reaction. Rejected any form of territorial internationalization of West Jerusalem. Expressed willingness to internationalize Holy Places.

Fate of Plan. Rejected by Ad Hoc Committee of U.N. General Assembly.

18. Archbishop of Canterbury's Plan of October 31, 1949. (Text discussion, p. 74.)

General Provisions. Dealt with Jerusalem.

Sovereignty over Jerusalem. Full territorial internationalization of Walled City and shopping areas immediately surrounding it. Rest of city to be incorporated into Israel.

Protection of Holy Places. Under protection of U.N.

Arab Reaction. Except for Jordan, Arabs called for full territorial internationalization of entire city. Jordan opposed any form of internationalization for East Jerusalem.

Jewish Reaction. Israel did not oppose internationalization of Walled City but rejected territorial internationalization of any part of West Jerusalem.

Fate of Plan. Not considered by U.N.

19. Israel Plan of 1949. (Text discussion, p. 75.)

General Provisions. U.N. Secretary General to conclude agreement with Israel guaranteeing protection of Holy Places in West Jerusalem.

Sovereignty over Jerusalem. West Jerusalem to be under Israeli sovereignty.

Protection of Holy Places. A U.N. representative to be appointed by Secretary General to reside in Jerusalem and observe implementation of agreement.

Arab Reaction. Except for Jordan, Arabs called for full territorial internationalization of city. Jordan opposed any form of internationalization in East Jerusalem.

Jewish Reaction. ---

Fate of Plan. Ad Hoc Committee of U.N. General Assembly adopted rival resolution.

20. Dutch-Swedish Proposal of 1949. (Text discussion, pp. 76-80.)

General Provisions. Functional internationalization of Holy Places.

Sovereignty over Jerusalem. Divided between Israel and Jordan.

Protection of Holy Places. Holy Places to be under supervision of a U.N. Commissioner.

Arab Reaction. Except for Jordan, Arabs called for full territorial internationalization of city. Jordan opposed any form of internationalization for East Jerusalem.

Jewish Reaction. Israel willing to accept it.

Fate of Plan. U.N. General Assembly adopted rival resolution.

21. U.N. General Assembly Resolution 303 (IV) of December 9, 1949. (Text discussion, pp. 74-80.)

General Provisions. Reaffirmed provision on Jerusalem contained in U.N. General Assembly Resolution 181 (II) of November 29, 1947.

Sovereignty over Jerusalem. Jerusalem to be established as a *corpus separatum* under a special international regime and to be administered by the United Nations.

Protection of Holy Places. Under United Nations protection.

Arab Reaction. Except for Jordan, resolution welcomed by Arabs. Jordan refused to accept any form of internationalization in East Jerusalem.

Jewish Reaction. Israel refused to accept territorial internationalization of West Jerusalem.

Fate of Plan. U.N. Trusteeship Council called upon to draft statute for Jerusalem.

22. Garreau Plan of January 1950. (Text discussion, pp. 82-84.)

General Provisions. Dealt with Jerusalem.

Sovereignty over Jerusalem. Jerusalem to be divided into three zones: an Israeli zone, a Jordanian zone, and an international zone.

Protection of Holy Places. Under supervision of U.N.

Arab Reaction. Except for Jordan, Arabs called for full territorial internationalization. Jordan opposed any form of internationalization in East Jerusalem.

Jewish Reaction. Israel did not oppose territorial internationalization of Walled City but rejected territorial internationalization of any part of West Jerusalem. Israel willing to discuss functional internationalization of Holy Places.

Fate of Plan. Shelved by U.N. Trusteeship Council.

23. Eban Plan of February 1950. (Text discussion, pp. 85-86.)

General Provisions. Dealt with Jerusalem.

Sovereignty over Jerusalem. Jerusalem to remain divided between Jordan and Israel.

Protection of Holy Places. A U.N. representative to have full control of Holy Places, including protection, free access, and repairs.

Arab Reaction. Except for Jordan, Arabs called for full territorial internationalization of Jerusalem. Jordan opposed any form of internationalization in East Jerusalem.

Jewish Reaction.

Fate of Plan. Rejected by Trusteeship Council.

24. Statute for Jerusalem. (Text discussion, pp. 84-90.)

General Provisions. Provided for government of Jerusalem.

Sovereignty over Jerusalem. Jerusalem to be *corpus separatum* under a special international regime and to be administered by the U.N.

Protection of Holy Places. Special concern of U.N. Governor of Jerusalem.

Arab Reaction. Except for Jordan, Arabs accepted it. Jordan opposed any form of internationalization for East Jerusalem.

Jewish Reaction. Israel opposed territorial internationalization of West Jerusalem.

Fate of Plan. Approved by U.N. Trusteeship Council on April 4, 1950. In light of Israeli and Jordanian opposition, Trusteeship Council declined to take further steps without instructions from U.N. General Assembly. Assembly never issued any instructions.

25. Israeli Stand in 1967-1968. (Text discussion, pp. 108-9.)

General Provisions. Jerusalem to be unified city under Israeli administration.

Sovereignty over Jerusalem. City to be under Israeli administration. Other details to be negotiated with Jordan.

Protection of Holy Places. Holy Places to be under control of those interested in them.

Arab Reaction. Arab states called for return of East Jerusalem to Jordanian hands.

Jewish Reaction.

Fate of Plan. Not yet known.

26. Arab States' Stand in 1967-1968. (Text discussion, p. 102.)

General Provisions. Return to *status quo ante* June 5, 1967.

Sovereignty over Jerusalem. East Jerusalem to be under Jordanian sovereignty.

Protection of Holy Places. Holy Places in East Jerusalem to be under Jordanian protection.

Arab Reaction.

Jewish Reaction. Israel called for negotiations. At the same time, Israeli officials said East Jerusalem would never be returned to Jordanian hands.

Fate of Plan. Not yet known.

Appendix C

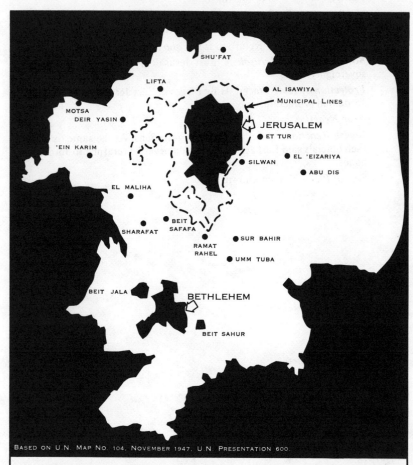

BASED ON U.N. MAP NO. 104, NOVEMBER 1947, U.N. PRESENTATION 600.

JERUSALEM INTERNATIONALIZED, THE CORPUS SEPARATUM

THE CITY OF JERUSALEM SHALL BE ESTABLISHED AS A **CORPUS SEPARATUM** UNDER A SPECIAL INTERNATIONAL REGIME AND SHALL BE ADMINISTERED BY THE UNITED NATIONS. THE TRUSTEESHIP COUNCIL SHALL BE DESIGNATED TO DISCHARGE THE RESPONSIBILITIES OF THE ADMINISTERING AUTHORITY ON BEHALF OF THE UNITED NATIONS.

THE CITY OF JERUSALEM SHALL INCLUDE THE PRESENT MUNICIPALITY OF JERUSALEM PLUS THE SURROUNDING VILLAGES AND TOWNS, THE MOST EASTERN OF WHICH SHALL BE ABU DIS; THE MOST SOUTHERN BETHLEHEM; THE MOST WESTERN 'EIN KARIM (INCLUDING ALSO THE BUILT-UP AREA OF MOTSA); AND THE MOST NORTHERN SHU'FAT, AS INDICATED ON THE ATTACHED SKETCH-MAP (ABOVE).

JERUSALEM ACCORDING TO THE U.N. PARTITION PLAN ADOPTED BY THE GENERAL ASSEMBLY, NOVEMBER 29, 1947. SECTIONS A AND B FROM PART III OF RESOLUTION 181(II)A.

140

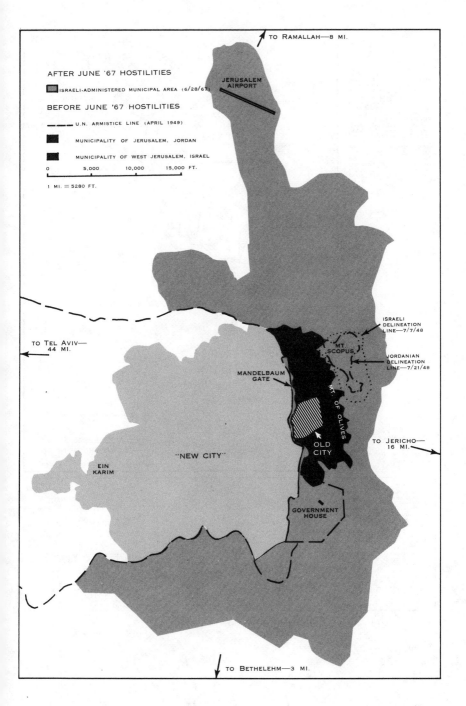

TO RAMALLAH—8 MI.

AFTER JUNE '67 HOSTILITIES

ISRAELI-ADMINISTERED MUNICIPAL AREA (6/28/67)

BEFORE JUNE '67 HOSTILITIES

U.N. ARMISTICE LINE (APRIL 1949)

MUNICIPALITY OF JERUSALEM, JORDAN

MUNICIPALITY OF WEST JERUSALEM, ISRAEL

0   5,000   10,000   15,000 FT.

1 MI. = 5280 FT.

JERUSALEM
AIRPORT

ISRAELI
DELINEATION
LINE—7/7/48

TO TEL AVIV—
44 MI.

MT.
SCOPUS

JORDANIAN
DELINEATION
LINE—7/21/48

MANDELBAUM
GATE

MT.
OF
OLIVES

"NEW CITY"

OLD
CITY

TO JERICHO—
16 MI.

EIN
KARIM

GOVERNMENT
HOUSE

TO BETHELEHM—3 MI.

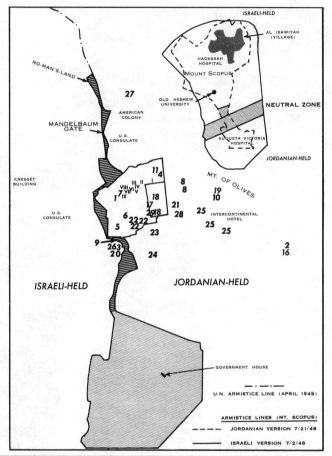

SITUATION PRIOR TO HOSTILITIES 1967

ACCORDING TO THE MOUNT SCOPUS AGREEMENT OF JULY 7, 1948, THE WHOLE OF THE MOUNT SCOPUS AREA WAS UNDER U.N. PROTECTION. THERE WAS ALSO A NO-MAN'S-LAND ALONG THE MAIN ROAD BETWEEN AUGUSTA VICTORIA HOSPITAL AND THE HEBREW UNIVERSITY BUILDINGS.

GOVERNMENT HOUSE AND THE SURROUNDING AREA WAS HANDED OVER TO THE UNITED NATIONS IN OCTOBER 1948 BY THE INTERNATIONAL RED CROSS IN PURSUANCE OF AN AGREEMENT WITH THE MANDATE POWER.

LIST OF HOLY PLACES TAKEN FROM U.N. MAP NO. 229, NOVEMBER 1949. U.N. PRESENTATION 1485.

Map labels: ISRAELI-HELD · AL ISAWIYAH (VILLAGE) · NO-MAN'S-LAND · HADASSAH HOSPITAL · MOUNT SCOPUS · OLD HEBREW UNIVERSITY · NEUTRAL ZONE · AMERICAN COLONY · MANDELBAUM GATE · U.S. CONSULATE · AUGUSTA VICTORIA HOSPITAL · JORDANIAN-HELD · KNESSET BUILDING · MT. OF OLIVES · U.S. CONSULATE · INTERCONTINENTAL HOTEL · ISRAELI-HELD · JORDANIAN-HELD · GOVERNMENT HOUSE

U.N. ARMISTICE LINE (APRIL 1949)

ARMISTICE LINES (MT. SCOPUS)
- – – – JORDANIAN VERSION 7/21/48
- ———— ISRAELI VERSION 7/2/48

CHRISTIAN	MUSLIM	JEWISH
1. BASILICA OF THE HOLY SEPULCHRE *		
2. BETHANY		
3. CENACLE		
4. CHURCH OF ST. ANNE		
5. CHURCH OF ST. JAMES THE GREAT		
6. CHURCH OF ST. MARK		20. TOMB OF DAVID (NEBI DAOUD)
7. DEIR AL SULTAN *		21. TOMB OF ABSALOM
8. TOMB OF THE VIRGIN * AND GARDEN OF GETHSEMANE		22. ANCIENT AND MODERN SYNAGOGUES
9. HOUSE OF CAIPHAS AND PRISON OF CHRIST		23. BATH OF RABBI ISHMAEL
10. SANCTUARY OF THE ASCENSION * AND MOUNT OF OLIVES		24. BROOK SILOAM
11. POOL OF BETHESDA		25. CEMETARY ON MOUNT OF OLIVES
12. 'EIN KARIM * *	16. TOMB OF LAZARUS	26. TOMB OF DAVID
13. BASILICA OF THE NATIVITY, BETHLEHEM * * *	17. EL BURAK ESH-SHARIF	27. TOMB OF SIMON THE JUST
14. MILK GROTTO, BETHLEHEM * * *	18. HAREM AL-SHARIF (MOSQUE OF UMAR AND MOSQUE OF ASKA)	28. TOMB OF ZACHARIAH AND OTHER TOMBS IN KIDRON VALLEY
15. SHEPHERDS FIELD, BETHLEHEM * * *	19. MOSQUE OF THE ASCENSION	29. WAILING WALL *
I TO IX INCLUSIVE. STATIONS OF THE CROSS		30. RACHAEL'S TOMB * * *

* HOLY PLACE TO WHICH THE STATUS QUO APPLIES.
* * HOLY PLACES IN INTERNATIONAL AREA OF JERUSALEM NOT SHOWN ON THIS MAP.

Notes

Chapter 1

[1]Texts of the two agreements may be found in J. C. Hurewitz, ed., *Diplomacy in the Near and Middle East*, Volume II, pp. 18-25.

[2]Great Britain, Parliamentary Papers, Cmd. 5957, p. 8.

[3]Great Britain, Parliamentary Papers, Cmd. 5479, Chapter II, para. 8. The vilayet of Beirut included the sanjaks of Acre and Balqa (Nablus), comprising Palestine west of the Jordan River and north of Jaffa. The independent sanjak of Jerusalem was comprised of Jaffa and Palestine south of the 32nd parallel and west of the Jordan and the Dead Sea. The southern boundary of the independent sanjak ran from the southern end of the Dead Sea to a point on the Egyptian boundary approximately midway between the Mediterranean Sea and the Gulf of Aqaba. For the argument that the "whole of Palestine West of the Jordan" was not excluded from the McMahon pledge, see Great Britain, Parliamentary Papers, Cmd. 5974, and George Antonius, *The Arab Awakening*, pp. 177-83.

[4]Great Britain, Foreign Office, *Documents on British Foreign Policy, 1919-1939*, 1st Series, Vol. IV, p. 251; David Lloyd George, *The Truth about the Peace Treaties*, Vol. II, p. 1038, 1089-91, and 1161-62; and Paul Mantoux, *Les Délibérations du Conseil des Quatre*, Vol. II, p. 159.

[5]Vatican overtures to France began shortly after the armistice in 1918, but relations were not officially restored until 1922. Maurice Pernod, *Le Saint-Siège, l'Eglise catholique, et la Politique mondiale*, pp. 76-78 and 81-82.

[6]*Ibid.*, pp. 82-83, 161-63, and 172-74.

[7]Leonard Stein, *The Balfour Declaration*, p. 409, note 56.

[8]Quoted in Constantine Rackauskas, *The Internationalization of Jerusalem*, p. 9.

[9]Great Britain, Foreign Office, *Documents on British Foreign Policy, 1919-1939*, 1st Series, Vol. VII, pp. 109-11; *ibid.*, Vol. VIII, pp. 159-71; and David Lloyd George, *The Truth about the Peace Treaties*, Vol. II, pp. 1162-75.

[10]The original French text is given in Great Britain, Foreign Office, *Documents on British Foreign Policy, 1919-1939*, 1st Series, Vol. VIII, p. 162. The English text given here came from Lloyd George, *The Truth about the Peace Treaties*, Vol. II, p. 1167.

[11]Paragraph 2, Article 95, of the Treaty of Sèvres read: "The Mandatory undertakes to appoint as soon as possible a special Commission to study and regulate all questions and claims relating to the different religious communities. In the composition of this Commission the religious interests concerned will be taken into account. The Chairman of the Commission will be appointed by the Council of the League of Nations." Great Britain, Parliamentary Papers, Cmd. 964, p. 26.

[12]Text found in the United States, Department of State, *Foreign Relations of the United States, 1921*, Vol. I, pp. 110-17.

[13]United States, Department of State, *Mandate for Palestine*, pp. 49-103.

[14]Great Britain, Parliamentary Papers, Cmd. 1708, p. 3. The text was subsequently modified by the Council of the League of Nations so that the language would match Article 5 of the Syrian mandate. See Document No. 711/78/65, Note dated August 2, 1922, from the British Foreign Office (Oliphant) to the American Ambassador (Harvey) in United States, Department of State, *Mandate for Palestine*, pp. 77-78. The text of the mandate instrument as approved by the League Council may be found in Great Britain, Parliamentary Papers, Cmd. 1785, *Mandate for Palestine*, pp. 2-9.

[15]Text in *The New York Times*, June 16, 1922.

[16]Stein, *The Balfour Declaration*, pp. 552-56; and Great Britain, Parliamentary Papers, Cmd. 5479, Chapter II, paras. 37-39.

[17]Great Britain, Parliamentary Papers, Cmd. 1700, p. 20.

[18]Great Britain, Parliamentary Papers, Cmd. 1708, p. 4.

[19]*Ibid.*, pp. 7-8.

[20]League of Nations, *Official Journal*, August 1922, pp. 817-23.

[21]*Ibid.*, p. 822.

[22]Text found in League of Nations, *Official Journal*, November 1922, pp. 1153-54.

[23]*The New York Times*, September 7, 1922.

[24]Yves de la Brière, *L'Organisation internationale du Monde contemporain et la Papauté souveraine*, première série, pp. 188-89; and Bernardin Collin, *Les Lieux-Saints*, p. 142.

[25]La Brière, *L'Organisation internationale, loc. cit.*

[26]The reason for the close relations was not entirely, or even primarily, political. The Vatican had rebuffed in 1896 an Anglican attempt at closer relations. The result was an ardent Anglican courtship of the Orthodox, which the latter found not unwelcome. John R. H. Moorman, *A History of the Church in England*, pp. 404-6; and Ruth Rouse and Stephen C. Neill, eds., *A History of the Ecumenical Movement, 1517-1948*, pp. 210-11 and 297-98.

[27]The Vatican was not particularly happy about the prospect of seeing Russian influence replaced by the enhanced prestige of the Phanar. Hence the Vatican favored the Turks. Pernod, *Le Saint Siège*, p. 180.

[28]*Ibid.*, pp. 116 and 119.

[29]Sir Anton Bertram and Harry Charles Luke, *Report of the Commission*, pp. 38-42.

[30]*Ibid.*, pp. 217-35.

[31]League of Nations, *Official Journal*, November 1922, pp. 1150-52.

[32]League of Nations, *Official Journal*, November 1923, pp. 1349 and 1355.

[33]The Palestine (Holy Places) Order in Council of 1924. The text may be found in Palestine, *Official Gazette*, No. 123, September 15, 1924, p. 814.

[34]League of Nations, Permanent Mandates Commission, *Minutes of the Sixteenth Session Held at Geneva from November 6 to 26, 1929*, pp. 198-99.

[35]*Ibid.*, pp. 143 and 156-71.

[36]League of Nations, *Official Journal*, February 1930, pp. 172-74.

[37]The text of the Ottoman Imperial Regulations (Fundamental Law of the Orthodox Patriarchate) of 1875 may be found in Sir Anton Bertram and J. W. A. Young, *The Orthodox Patriarchate of Jerusalem; Commission's Report on Certain Controversies*, pp. 291-300.

[38]*Ibid.*, pp. 252-69.

[39]*Ibid.*, pp. 291-316.

[40]*Ibid.*, pp. 221-25.

[41]*The New York Times*, July 24, 1935, and *The Times*, July 23 and July 25, 1935.

[42]*The Times*, October 16, 1939.

[43]Orthodox Patriarchate Ordinance, 1941. See *The Palestine Gazette*, No. 1142 (November 20, 1941), p. 1151, and Supplement No. 1.

Chapter 2

[1]Great Britain, Colonial Office, Colonial No. 133, pp. 1-2.

[2]See Great Britain, Colonial Office, Colonial No. 134, pp. 292-99.

[3]Great Britain, Parliamentary Papers, Cmd. 5479, Chapter V, para. 64.

[4]*Ibid.*

[5]*Ibid.*, Chapter XVIII, para. 10.

[6]*Ibid.*, Chapter XVIII, para. 11.

[7]*Ibid.*, Chapter II, para. 39.

[8]*Ibid.*, Chapter XXII, paras. 10 and 12.

[9]Great Britain, Parliamentary Papers, Cmd. 5513.

[10]Great Britain, Parlaimentary Papers, Cmd. 5854, p. 16.

[11]League of Nations, Permanent Mandates Commission, *Minutes of the Thirty-Second (Extraordinary) Session Devoted to Palestine Held at Geneva from July 30 to August 18, 1937*, p. 903.

[12]League of Nation, *Official Journal*, December 1937, p. 902.

[13]*Ibid.*, p. 903.

[14]League of Nations, Permanent Mandates Commission, *Minutes of the Thirty-second (Extraordinary) Session*, p. 173; and John Bagot Glubb, *Britain and the Arabs*, p. 153.

[15]Text found in Great Britain, Parliamentary Papers, Cmd. 5854, pp. 18-19.

[16]Text in *New Judaea*, August-September 1937, pp. 235-36.

[17]Text in Great Britain, Parliamentary Papers, Cmd. 5854, p. 73.

[18]Department of State, *Foreign Relations of the United States*, 1937, Vol. II, pp. 891-914.

[19]Department of State, Press Releases, Vol. XIX, No. 472 (October 15, 1938), pp. 260-61.

[20]*The Public Papers and Addresses of Franklin D. Roosevelt*, Vol. VIII (1938), pp. 550-51.

[21]Great Britain, Parliamentary Papers, Cmd. 5854.

[22]*Ibid.*

[23]*Ibid.*, pp. 243-46.

[24]Great Britain, Parliamentary Papers, Cmd. 6019.

[25]League of Nations, Permanent Mandates Commission, *Minutes of the Thirty-sixth Session Held at Geneva from June 8 to June 29, 1939*, pp. 94-246.

[26]*Ibid.*, pp. 274-75.

[27]Frank E. Manuel, *The Realities of American-Palestine Relations*, pp. 68-71.

Chapter 3

[1]Text of report in *The New York Times*, September 30, 1945.

[2]United States, Department of State, *Anglo-American Committee of Inquiry; Report to the United States Government and His Majesty's Government in the United Kingdom.*

[3]*The New York Times*, July 26, 1946; and Great Britain, Parliamentary Papers, Cmd. 7044, pp. 1-8.

[4]*The New York Times*, October 24, 1946.

[5]*The New York Times*, October 7, 1946; Christopher Sykes, *Crossroads to Israel*, pp. 303-4; Joseph B. Schechtman, *The United States and the Jewish State Movement*, p. 177; J. C. Hurewitz, *The Struggle for Palestine*, pp. 264-65; Francis Williams, *A Prime Minister Remembers*, pp. 186-87; and Walter Millis, ed., *The Forrestal Diaries*, pp. 309-10; *cf.* Harry Truman, *Memoirs*, Vol. II, p. 154.

[6]*The New York Times*, October 5, 1946.

[7]United Nations, *Official Records of the First Special Session of the General Assembly*, Vol. III, First Committee, 52nd meeting.

[8]United Nations, *Official Records of the First Special Session of the General Assembly, Resolutions*, 106 (S-1).

[9]United Nations, A/364.

[10]Australia supported neither the majority plan nor the minority plan and abstained in the Special Committee's vote on the two plans. Herbert V. Evatt, *The Task of Nations*, p. 131.

[11]United Nations, *Official Records of the Second Session of the General Assembly, Plenary Meetings*, Vol. I, 91st meeting.

[12]United Nations, *Official Records of the Second Session of the General Assembly, Ad Hoc Committee on the Palestinian Question*, 3rd meeting.

[13]*Ibid.*, 4th Meeting.

[14]*Ibid.*, Annexes 19 and 19a.

[15]*Ibid.*, Annex 25.

[16]*Ibid.*, 32nd, 33rd, and 34th meetings.

[17]*Ibid.*, 28th meeting.

[18]*Ibid.*, 26th meeting.

[19]*In favor*: Australia, Bolivia, Brazil, Byelorussia, Canada, Chile, Costa Rica, Czechoslovakia, Denmark, Dominican Republic, Ecuador, Guatemala, Iceland, Nicaragua, Norway, Panama, Peru, Poland, South Africa, Sweden, the Ukraine, the U.S.S.R., the United States, Uruguay, Venezuela. *Against*: Afghanistan, Cuba, Egypt, India, Iran, Iraq, Lebanon,

Pakistan, Saudi Arabia, Siam, Syria, Turkey, Yemen. *Abstaining*: Argentina, Belgium, China, Columbia, El Salvador, Ethiopia, France, Greece, Haiti, Honduras, Liberia, Luxembourg, Mexico, the Netherlands, New Zealand, the United Kingdom, Yugoslavia. *Absent*: Paraguay, he Philippines. *Ibid.*, 34th meeting.

[20]*In favor*: Australia, Belgium, Bolivia, Brazil, Byelorussia, Canada, Costa Rica, Czechoslovakia, Denmark, Dominican Republic, Ecuador, France, Guatemala, Haiti, Iceland, Liberia, Luxembourg, the Netherlands, New Zealand, Nicaragua, Norway, Panama, Paraguay, Peru, the Philippines, Poland, South Africa, Sweden, the Ukraine, the U.S.S.R., the United States, Uruguay, Venezuela. *Against*: Afghanistan, Cuba, Egypt, Greece, India, Iran, Iraq, Lebanon, Pakistan, Saudi Arabia, Syria, Turkey, Yemen. *Abstaining*: Argentina, Chile, China, Colombia, El Salvador, Ethiopia, Honduras, Mexico, the United Kingdom, Yugoslavia. United Nations, *Official Records of the Second Session of the General Assembly, Plenary Meetings*, Vol. II, 128th meeting.

[21]Out of a total population of 205,000, about 40,000 were Christian. See United Nations, A/1286, p. 13.

[22]United Nations, Trusteeship Council, *Official Records; Second Session; Second Part*, 23rd meeting; and United Nations, T/118, Article 20.

[23]United Nations, T/118.

[24]The Trusteeship Council in 1948 was composed of Australia, Belgium, China, Costa Rica, France, Iraq, Mexico, New Zealand, the Philippines, the U.S.S.R., the U.K., and the U.S. The U.S.S.R. boycotted the Trusteeship Council from March 1947 until April 25, 1948, when Semyon Tsarapkin was named as the Soviet delegate to the Council.

[25]United Nations, Trusteeship Council, *Official Records; Second Session; Second Part*, 19th meeting.

[26]United Nations, T/123.

[27]United Nations, Trusteeship Council, *Official Records; Second Session; Second Part*, 23rd meeting.

[28]*Ibid.*, 24th meeting.

[29]*Ibid.*, 29th and 30th meetings.

[30]*Ibid.*, 35th meeting.

[31]United Nations, A/532.

[32]Truman, *Memoirs*, Vol. II, p. 162; and Millis, ed., *The Forrestal Diaries*, pp. 376-77.

[33]Trygve Lie, *In the Cause of Peace*, p. 171.

[34]United Nations, A/620, p. 81.

[35]United Nations, *Official Records of the Second Special Session of the General Assembly*, Vol. I, 132nd meeting; and United Nations, A/555, Resolution 185 (S-2).

[36]United Nations, A/544.

[37]United Nations, A/555, Resolution 187 (S-2).

[38]United Nations, *Official Records of the Second Special Session of the General Assembly*, Annex A/C.1/298.

[39]*Ibid.*, A/C.1/299.

[40]United Nations, *Official Records of the Second Special Session of the General Assembly*, Vol. II, First Committee, 140th meeting.

[41]*Ibid.*, Vol. I, 135th meeting.

[42]United Nations, A/555, Resolution 186 (S-2).

Chapter 4

[1]It is commonly believed that the name of the Hashimite Kingdom was changed from Transjordan to Jordan sometime in 1949. However, the change was made on May 25, 1946, when the country became independent and Abdallah was proclaimed king. The Parliament decided that the country should be known as al-Mamlakah al-Urdunniyyah al-Hashimiyyah; the Constitution, which was signed by King Abdallah on December 7, 1946, and took effect on March 1, 1947, gives this as the official name of the kingdom. See *al-Jaridah al-Rasmiyyah lil-Mamlakah al-Urdunniyyah al-Hashimiyyah*, No. 886 of February 1, 1947 (Jordan's Official Gazette). Public Notice No. 2, dated June 1, 1949, reminded the foreign legations in Amman, the Jordanian legations in foreign countries, and the Secretary General of the U.N. that the name of the kingdom was al-Mamlakah al-Urdunniyyah al-Hashimiyyah in Arabic and the Hashimite Kingdom of the Jordan in English. *See al-Jaridah al-Rasmiyyah lil-Mamlakah al-Urdunniyyah al-Hashimiyyah,* No. 984 of June 1, 1949.

[2]United Nations, S/743.

[3]Dr. Pablo de Azcárate y Florez, *Mission in Palestine, 1948-1952*, p. 50.

[4]United Nations, A/648, pp. 7-8.

[5]*Ibid.*, pp. 9-10.

[6]Folke Bernadotte, *To Jerusalem*, p. 12.

[7]United Nations, S/863, pp. 2-3.

[8]Dov Joseph, *The Faithful City*, p. 18.

[9]United Nations, A/519, Resolution 181 (II) A of November 29, 1947, Part III, Section D.

[10]Walter Eytan, *The First Ten Years*, p. 69.

[11]Joseph, *The Faithful City*, p. 334.

[12]Zeev Sharef, *Three Days*, p. 158.

[13]*Ibid.*, pp. 161-62.

[14]Joseph, *The Faithful City*, p. 334.

[15]United Nations, A/648, p. 25.

[16]United Nations, Security Council, *Official Records, Third Year*, No. 93, 331st meeting (July 7, 1948).

[17]Joseph, *The Faithful City*, pp. 298-99.

[18]*Iton Rishmi* (Official Gazette of the Provisional Government of Israel), No. 12, August 2, 1948, p. 66.

[19]*Ibid.*, p. 67.

[20]Ahmad Hilmi had been appointed Military Governor of Jordanian-held Jerusalem on July 1, 1948. See *al-Jaridah al-Rasmiyyah lil-Mamlakah al-Urdunniyyah al-Hashimiyyah*, No. 951, 1948.

[21]*The New York Times*, December 2, 1948.

[22]*Ibid.*, December 14, 1948.

[23]United Nations, A/648.

[24]Harry Truman, *Memoirs*, Vol. II, p. 166.

[25]The text may be found in *The New York Times*, October 29, 1948.

[26]Lillie Shultz, "The Jerusalem Story," *The Nation*, December 17, 1949, pp. 589-91.

[27]Original Latin text in *Oriente Moderno*, Vol. XXVIII, October-December 1948, pp. 172-74. Translated text in *The New York Times*, October 24, 1948.

[28]*The New York Times*, October 24, 1948.

[29]United Nations, *Official Records of the Third Session of the General Assembly, Part I, First Committee*, 215th meeting and 222nd meeting.

[30]*Ibid.*, 214th meeting.

[31]*Ibid.*, 228th meeting.

[32]Resolution 194 (III) of December 11, 1948, para. 8.

[33]The armistice agreements: *Israel-Egypt*, United Nations, S/1264/Rev. 1. *Israel-Lebanon*, United Nations, S/1296/Rev. 1. *Israel-Jordan*, United Nations, S/1302/Rev. 1. *Israel-Syria*, United Nations, S/1353/Rev. 1.

[34]*Iton Rishmi* (Official Gazette of the Provisional Government of Israel), No. 48, February 4, 1949.

[35]The armistice lines followed the lines under the truce signed on November 30, 1948, by Abdallah al-Tall on behalf of Jordan and Moshe Dayan on behalf of Israel.

[36]General Administration of Palestine Law No. 17, enacted March 14, 1949, and published in the official gazette on March 16. See *al-Jaridah al-Rasmiyyah lil-Mamlakah al-Urdunniyyah al-Hashimiyyah*, No. 975, 1949.

Chapter 5

[1]Resolution 194 (III) of December 11, 1948, para. 6.

[2]Joseph B. Keenan had been appointed by President Truman on December 28 to be the U.S. member on the Commission, but he resigned on January 14 and was replaced by Mark Ethridge. Mr. Ethridge was succeeded by Paul A. Porter on July 16, and Ely Elliot Palmer was appointed on November 4, 1949, to replace Porter.

[3]United Nations, A/838, para. 15.

[4]*Ibid.*, para. 28.

[5]United Nations, *Official Records of the Third Session of the General Assembly, Part II; Ad Hoc Political Committee*, 45th meeting.

[6]Benjamin Shwadran, "Jerusalem Again," *Middle Eastern Affairs*, Vol. I, No. 12 (December 1950), pp. 358-59.

[7]Original Latin text in *Oriente Moderno*, Vol. XXIX, April-June 1949, pp. 52-53. Translated text in *The New York Times*, April 16, 1949.

[8]James G. McDonald, *My Mission in Israel*, pp. 187-88 and 191-92.

[9]United Nations, *Official Records of the Fourth Session of the General Assembly; Ad Hoc Political Committee*, Annex, Vol. I, A/973 and A/973/Add. 1.

[10]Article 5. *Ibid.*, A/973.

[11]*The New York Times*, September 17, 1949.

[12]*The New York Times*, October 9, 1949.

[13]Walter Eytan, *The First Ten Years*, pp. 42-43; and James G. McDonald, *My Mission in Israel, 1948-1951*, pp. 192-96.

[14]Some writers have reported Abdallah as saying he would be willing to agree to internationalization of Jerusalem if Israel withdrew to the territory allotted it by the partition plan of 1947. It is unlikely, however, that Abdallah thought this was a serious possibility. See George Kirk, *The Middle East, 1945-1950*, p. 306.

[15]United Nations, A/1286, pp. 9-11; and *The New York Times*, November 27, 1949.

[16]Lillie Shultz, "The Jerusalem Story," *The Nation*, December 17, 1949, pp. 589-91.

[17]United Nations, *Official Records of the Fourth Session of the General Assembly; Ad Hoc Political Committee*, Annex, Vol. I, A/AC.31/L.37.

[18]*Ibid.*, A/AC.31/L.41.

[19]*Ibid.*, A/AC.31/L.42.

[20]*Ibid.*, Summary Records, 44th meeting.

[21]*Ibid.*, 43rd meeting.

[22]*Ibid.*, 48th meeting.

[23]The vote was 9-6-2. *In favor*: Australia, Egypt, El Salvador, Greece, Iraq, Lebanon, Peru, the Ukraine, the U.S.S.R. *Against*: Cuba, Israel, Mexico, the Netherlands, Sweden Uruguay. *Abstentions*: Canada, India. *Ibid.*, Annex, Vol. I, A/AC.31/11.

[24]*Ibid.*, A/AC.31/L.53.

[25]*Ibid.*, A/AC.31/L.54 and A/AC.31/L.57.

[26]*Ibid.*, A/AC.31/L.52.

[27]*Ibid.*, Summary Records, 57th meeting.

[28]*Ibid.*, 58th meeting.

[29]*Ibid.*

[30]*Ibid.*, 59th meeting.

[31]*Ibid.*, 57th and 58th meetings.

[32]*Ibid.*, 60th meeting.

[33]*In favor*: Afghanistan, Argentina, Austria, Belgium, Bolivia, Brazil, Burma, Byelorussia, China, Colombia, Costa Rica, Cuba, Czechoslovakia, Denmark, Ecuador, Egypt, El Salvador, France, Greece, Honduras, Iran, Iraq, Lebanon, Liberia, Luxembourg, Nicaragua, Pakistan, Paraguay, Peru, Poland, Saudi Arabia, Syria, the Ukraine, the U.S.S.R., Yemen. *Against*: Chile, Guatemala, Haiti, Iceland, Israel, Norway, South Africa, Sweden, Turkey, the U.K., the U.S. *Abstaining*: Canada, Dominican Republic, Ethiopia, India, Mexico, the Netherlands, New Zealand, Panama, the Philippines, Thailand, Venezuela. *Ibid.*, 61st meeting.

[34]United Nations, A/1227.

[35]United Nations, *Official Records of the Fourth Session of the General Assembly; Plenary Meetings*, 274th meeting.

[36]*Ibid.*, 275th meeting.

[37]*Ibid.*

[38]*Ibid.*, 274th and 275th meetings.

[39]United Nations, A/1231, *Palestine; Telegram from the Minister for Foreign Affairs of the Hashemite Kingdom of Jordan Addressed to the Secretary General.* Jordan not being a member of the United Nations, the Jordanian representative could not address the General Assembly.

[40]*In favor*: Afghanistan, Argentina, Australia, Belgium, Bolivia, Brazil, Burma, Byelorussia, China, Colombia, Cuba, Czechoslovakia, Ecuador, Egypt, El Salvador, Ethiopia, France, Greece, Haiti, India, Iran, Iraq, Lebanon, Liberia, Luxembourg, Mexico, Nicaragua, Pakistan, Paraguay, Peru, the Philippines, Poland, Saudi Arabia, Syria, the Ukraine, the U.S.S.R., Venezuela, Yemen. *Against*: Canada, Costa Rica, Denmark, Guatemala, Iceland, Israel, Norway, Sweden, South Africa, Turkey, the U.K., the U.S., Uruguay, Yugoslavia. *Abstaining*: Chile, Dominican Republic, Honduras, the Netherlands, New Zealand, Panama, Thailand. United Nations, *Official Records of the Fourth Session of the General Assembly of the United Nations; Plenary Meetings*, 275th meeting.

[41]*The Jerusalem Post*, November 27, 1964.

[42]*The New York Times*, December 11, 1949.

[43]Text of Ben-Gurion's statement found in *The Jerusalem Post*, November 27, 1964.

[44]*The New York Times*, August 3, 1949.

[45]*Al-Jaridah al-Rasmiyyah lil-Mamlakah al-Urdunniyyah al-Hashimiyyah*, No. 420, 1949.

[46]*Ibid.*, No. 420 and No. 421, 1949.

[47]United Nations, Trusteeship Council, *Official Records; Second Special Session*, 4th meeting.

[48]*Ibid.*, 5th meeting.

[49]*Ibid.*

[50]*Ibid.*, 7th meeting.

[51]*Ibid.*, 8th meeting.

[52]*The Jewish Agency's Digest of Press and Events*, Vol. II, No. 18 (January 27, 1950), p. 790.

[53]Israel, Knesset, *Divrei Haknesset*, 2nd session, No. 11, 1950, p. 603.

[54]Document T/457. See United Nations, A/1286, pp. 3-18.

[55]*Ibid.*, para. 6.

[56]United Nations, Trusteeship Council, *Official Records; Fourth Year; Sixth Session*, 9th meeting.

[57]*Ibid.*, 18th meeting. The Orthodox Patriarchate has maintained that it is a monastic organization and that this monastic system is guaranteed by the status quo of 1852.

[58]*Ibid.*, 20th meeting.

[59]*Ibid.*, 19th meeting.

[60]*Ibid.*, 28th meeting.

[61]*Ibid.*

[62]*Ibid.*

[63]United Nations, Trusteeship Council, *Official Records; Fourth Year; Sixth Session; Annex*, Vol. I, T/L.36.

[64]United Nations, Trusteeship Council, *Official Records; Fourth Year; Sixth Session*, 43rd meeting.

[65]*Ibid.*

[66]United Nations, Trusteeship Council, *Official Records; Fourth Year; Sixth Session; Annex*, Vol. I, T/L.53.

[67]Article 30. The Statute for the City of Jerusalem may be found in United Nations, A/1286, pp. 19-27.

[68]*Majmu'at al-Qawanin wa al-Anzimah* (Collection of Laws and Regulations), Vol. I, p. 4.

[69]United Nations Map No. 229, November 1949.
[70]United Nations, A/1286, p. 30.
[71]*Ibid.*
[72]United Nations, A/AC.38/L.63.
[73]United Nations, A/AC.38/L.71.
[74]United Nations, *Official Records of the Fifth Session of the General Assembly; Ad Hoc Political Committee*, 81st meeting.
[75]The vote was 30 in favor, 18 against, and 9 abstentions. *In favor*: Afghanistan, Argentina, Belgium, Bolivia, Brazil, Burma, Chile, China, Colombia, Cuba, Dominican Republic, Ecuador, Egypt, Ethiopia, France, Greece, Indonesia, Iran, Iraq, Lebanon, Luxembourg, Pakistan, Panama, Paraguay, Peru, the Philippines, Saudi Arabia, Syria, Venezuela, and Yemen. *Against*: Australia, Denmark, Guatemala, Honduras, Iceland, Israel, the Netherlands, New Zealand, Nicaragua, Norway, South Africa, Sweden, Thailand, Turkey, the U.K., the U.S., Uruguay, and Yugoslavia. *Abstentions*: Byelorussia, Canada, Costa Rica, Czechoslovakia, India, Mexico, Poland, the Ukraine, and the U.S.S.R. United Nations, *Official Records of the Fifth Session of the General Assembly; Plenary Meetings*, 326th meeting.

Chapter 6

[1]*The Times*, December 5, 1953.
[2]Walter Eytan, *The First Ten Years*, p. 83.
[3]*The Times*, November 11, 1954; and *The New York Times*, November 13, 1954.
[4]*The New York Times*, November 4, 1954.
[5]*Ibid.*, November 5, 1954.
[6]The text of the U.S. aide memoire delivered to Israel on July 9, 1952, may be found in Department of State Press Release No. 576, July 22, 1952.
[7]Eytan, *The First Ten Years*, p. 81.
[8]*In Jerusalem*: Bolivia, Central African Republic, Chile, Colombia, Congo (Brazzaville), Congo (Kinshasa), Costa Rica, Dahomey, Dominican Republic, Gabon, Greece, Guatemala, Honduras, Ivory Coast, Malagasy Republic, the Netherlands, Niger, Panama, Upper Volta, Uruguay, and Venezuela. *In the Tel Aviv area*: Argentina, Australia, Austria, Belgium, Brazil, Bulgaria, Burma, Canada, Cuba, Czechoslovakia, Denmark, Ecuador, Finland, France, Germany (West), Ghana, Great Britain, Hungary, Italy, Japan, Liberia, Mexico, Norway, Peru, the Philippines, Poland, Romania, Sweden, Switzerland, Turkey, the U.S.S.R., the U.S., and Yugoslavia. *Israel Government Year Book 1966-1967*, pp. 168-72.
[9]*The Jerusalem Post*, January 25, 1963.
[10]The text of the diploma of appointment is given in King Abdallah of Jordan, *My Memoirs Completed (al-Takmilah)*, Appendix A.
[11]United Nations, S/1302/Rev. 1.
[12]Israel, Ministry for Foreign Affairs, *Desecration*.
[13]Katherine W. Sellers, "Armenian Church Torn by Dispute," *The Christian Century*, Vol. LXXIV, No. 51 (December 18, 1957), pp. 1522-24.

[14]*The New York Times*, October 11, 1956.

[15]Sellers, *loc. cit.*

[16]*Ibid.*

[17]*Ibid.*

[18]*The New York Times*, September 1, 1958.

[19]*Ibid.*, January 30, 1957.

[20]*The Times*, March 12, 1957.

[21]L. G. A. Cust, *The Status Quo in the Holy Places*, p. 30.

[22] I. L. Kenen, ed., "The Future of Jerusalem," *Near East Report*, January 1968, Supplement, p. 15a.

[23]*Maariv*, June 3, 1966.

[24]Speech by U.A.R. President Nasser to U.A.R. troops in Sinai on May 22, 1967; speech by President Nasser at Cairo University Hall on July 23, 1967; and *The Washington Post*, July 25, 1967.

[25]Drew Pearson and Jack Anderson, "Hussein Declined Immunity Offer," *The Washington Post*, June 21, 1967; and Israel Information Services, *Jordanian Belligerency*, pp. 1-2.

[26]United Nations, A/6717, A/L.519, A/PV.1527, and A/PV.1529.

[27]*The New York Times*, June 13, 1967; and *The Washington Post*, June 13, 1967.

[28]United States, Department of State, *United States Policy in the Near East Crisis*, pp. 16-18.

[29]*Ibid.*, p. 17.

[30]United Nations, A/PV.1525.

[31]United Nations, S/PV.1382 and S/RES/242 (1967).

[32]Those expelled from the Jewish quarter and the Maghribi quarter were subsequently compensated in one form or another. *The New York Times*, January 10, 1968; and United Nations, S/8146, p. 9.

[33]Law and Administration Ordinance (Amendment No. 11) Law, 5727-1967. The text may be found in Israel, *Sefer Hachukkim*, No. 499, June 28, 1967, p. 74.

[34]Municipal Corporations Ordinance (Amendment No. 7) Law, 5727-1967. The text may be found *ibid.*

[35]Protection of Holy Places Law, 5727-1967. The text may be found *ibid.*, p. 75.

[36]Jerusalem (Enlargement of Municipal Area) Proclamation, 5727-1967. The text may be found in Israel, *Kovetz Hatakanot*, No. 2065, June 28, 1967, pp. 2694-95.

[37]*The New York Times*, June 30, 1967; and *The Washington Post*, June 30, 1967.

[38]*The New York Times*, July 1, 1967.

[39]The text of the statement by the Department of State spokesman may be found in United States, Department of State, *Transcript of Press and Radio News Briefing*, June 28, 1967.

[40]The vote was 99-0, with 20 abstentions. Those abstaining were: Australia, Barbados, Bolivia, Central African Republic, Colombia, Congo (Kinshasa), Dahomey, Gabon, Iceland, Italy, Jamaica, Kenya, Liberia, Malawi, Malta, Portugal, Rwanda, South Africa, the U.S., and Uruguay. United Nations, A/PV.1548, pp. 102-5.

[41]The text of the letter is found in *The New York Times*, July 12, 1967.

[42]*The New York Times*, July 12, 1967.

[43]*Ibid.*, July 15, 1967.

[44]*Ibid.*, August 24, 1967.

[45]*The Washington Post*, July 10 and September 9, 1967.

[46]*The New York Times*, June 27, 1967.

[47]*Ibid.*, July 13, 1967.

[48]*The Washington Post*, July 27, 1967.

[49]Again the vote was 99-0. There were 18 abstentions: Australia, Barbados, Bolivia, Central African Republic, Colombia, Congo (Kinshasa) Iceland, Jamaica, Kenya, Liberia, Malagasy Republic, Malawi, Malta, Portugal, Rwanda, South Africa, the U.S., and Uruguay. United Nations, A/PV. 1554, p. 41. The text of the resolution may be found in United Nations, A/L.5281/Rev. 2.

[50]*The New York Times*, July 15, 1967.

[51]Republican Coordinating Committee, *The Middle East—Crisis and Opportunity*, pp. 2-3.

[52]*The New York Times*, November 28, 1967.

[53]*Ibid.*, July 20, 1967.

[54]*The Washington Post*, August 3, 1967.

[55]They were required to pay the difference between the lower Jordanian customs, which they had already paid, and the higher Israeli customs figures. United Nations, S/8146, p. 13.

[56]*Haaretz*, August 18, 1967; and United Nations, S/3146, p. 39. The account of David's purchase is found in II Samuel XXIV: 18-25.

[57]United Nations, S/8146, p. 7.

[58]*The New York Times*, January 12, 1968; and *The Jerusalem Post*, January 12, 1968.

Chapter 7

[1]*The New York Times*, July 10, 1950.

[2]International Commission for the Wailing Wall, *Report of the Commission . . . to Determine the Rights and Claims of Moslems and Jews in Connection with the Western or Wailing Wall at Jerusalem*, p. 24.

[3]Resolution 194 (III), para. 9.

[4]Richard Hartmann, *Palästina unter den Arabern*, p. 34.

[5]Michael Avi-Yonah, David H. K. Amiran, Julius Jotham Rothschild, and H. M. Z. Meyer, *Jerusalem, The Saga of the Holy City*, p. 40.

[6]I. P. Warren, *Jerusalem Ancient and Modern*, pp. 46-47; and Frank E. Manuel, *The Realities of American-Palestine Relations*, p. 13.

[7]United Nations, *Official Records of the Fifth Session of the General Assembly; Supplement No. 9* (A/1286), p. 17.

[8]*Ibid.*, p. 12.

Bibliography

A. Documents, Records, Reports, and Official Publications

1. Great Britain

Colonial Office. Colonial No. 133. *Palestine Royal Commission; Memoranda Prepared by the Government of Palestine.* London: H. M. Stationery Office, 1937.

––––––. Colonial No. 134. *Palestine Royal Commission; Minutes of Evidence Heard at Public Sessions.* London: H. M. Stationery Office, 1937.

Foreign Office. *Documents on British Foreign Policy. 1919-1939.* 1st Series. Vol. IV, VII, and VIII. London: H. M. Stationery Office, 1919, 1920, and 1958.

Parliamentary Papers. Cmd. 964. Treaty Series No. 11 (1920). *Treaty of Peace with Turkey.* London: H. M. Stationery Office, 1920.

––––––. Cmd. 1700. *British Policy in Palestine.* London: H. M. Stationery Office, 1922.

––––––. Cmd. 1708. *Mandate for Palestine; Letter from the Secretary to the Cabinet to the Secretary-General of the League of Nations of July 1, 1922, Enclosing a Note in Reply to Cardinal Gasparri's Letter of May 15, 1922, Addressed to the Secretary-General of the League of Nations.* London: H. M. Stationery Office, 1922.

––––––. Cmd. 1785. *Mandate for Palestine.* London: H. M. Stationery Office, 1922.

––––––. Cmd. 5479. *Palestine Royal Commission Report.* London: H. M. Stationery Office, 1937.

––––––. Cmd. 5513. *Palestine; Statement of Policy.* London: H. M. Stationery Office, 1937.

––––––. Cmd. 5854. *Palestine Partition Commission Report.* London: H. M. Stationery Office, 1938.

––––––. Cmd. 5957. *Correspondence between Sir Henry McMahon, His Majesty's High Commissioner at Cairo and the Sherif Hussein of Mecca.* London: H. M. Stationery Office, 1939.

––––––. Cmd. 5974. *Report of a Committee Set Up to Consider Certain Correspondence between Sir Henry McMahon and the Sharif of Mecca in 1915 and 1916.* London: H. M. Stationery Office, 1939.

––––––. Cmd. 6019. *Palestine; Statement of Policy.* London: H. M. Stationery Office, 1939.

––––––. Cmd. 7044. *Proposals for the Future of Palestine.* London: H. M. Stationery Office, 1947.

2. Israel

Israel Government Year Book. 1966-1967. Jerusalem: Government Printer, 1966.

Iton Rishmi (Official Gazette of the Provisional Government of Israel). Tel Aviv: 1948-1949.

Jerusalem, 1948-1951. Jerusalem: Government Printer, 1952.

Jerusalem, Living City. Jerusalem: Government Printer, 1950.

Kovetz Hatakkanot. No. 2065. Jerusalem: Government Printer, June 28, 1967.

Laws of the State of Israel; Authorized Translation from the Hebrew. Jerusalem: Government Printer, 1948-. Annual.

Sefer Hachukkim. No. 499. Jerusalem: Government Printer, June 28, 1967.

Central Bureau of Statistics. *Statistical Abstract of Israel.* 1949-1950, 1952-1953, and 1958-1959. Jerusalem: Government Printer, 1950, 1953, and 1959.

————. *Statistical Abstract of Israel.* 1962, 1966, and 1967. Jerusalem: Central Bureau of Statistics, 1962, 1966, and 1967.

Information Services. *Jordanian Belligerency.* New York, November 1967.

Knesset. *Divrei Haknesset.* 2nd session. No. 11, 1950. Jerusalem: Government Printer, 1950.

Ministry for Foreign Affairs. *Desecration.* Jerusalem: Government Printer, November 1967.

————. *Jerusalem: One and Eternal.* Jerusalem: Ministry for Foreign Affairs, 1967.

Mission to the United Nations. *Memorandum on the Future of Jerusalem; An Analysis of the Palestine Conciliation Commission's Draft Instrument Submitted to the General Assembly of the United Nations.* Lake Success, November 15, 1949.

Office of Information. *Jerusalem and the United Nations.* New York: Israel Office of Information, 1953.

————. *The Peace of Jerusalem; Texts of Addresses Presenting the Position of the Government of Israel on the Future of Jerusalem, during the Fourth Session of the General Assembly of the United Nations, 1949.* New York: Israel Office of Information, 1950.

3. Jewish Agency for Palestine

Digest of Press and Events. Vol. II (1950). Jerusalem: The Jewish Agency, 1950.

The Jewish Case before the Anglo-American Committee of Inquiry on Palestine. Jerusalem: The Jewish Agency for Palestine, 1947.

The Jewish Plan for Palestine; Memoranda and Statements Presented by the Jewish Agency for Palestine to the United Nations Special Committee on Palestine. Jerusalem: The Jewish Agency for Palestine, 1947.

The Political Problem of Palestine; An Analysis of Proposed Solutions. Jerusalem: The Jewish Agency for Palestine, July 1947.

Statistical Handbook of Jewish Palestine. Jerusalem: The Jewish Agency for Palestine, 1947.

4. Jordan

Al-Jaridah al-Rasmiyyah lil-Mamlakah al-Urdunniyyah al-Hashimiyyah (Official Gazette of the Hashimite Kingdom of Jordan). Amman: 1946-1950.

Department of Statistics. *First Census of Population and Housing. 18 November, 1961; Interim Report No. 7: Distribution and Characteristics of Population, Jerusalem District.* Amman: The Statistical Department Press, May 1963.

5. *League of Nations*

Official Journal. Geneva, 1922, 1923, 1930, 1937, 1939.
Permanent Mandates Commission. *Minutes.* 16th session. Geneva, 1929.
————. *Minutes.* 29th-37th sessions. Geneva, 1936-1939.

6. *Palestine*

Official Gazette. Jerusalem: Government Printer, 1922-1932.
Palestine Gazette. Jerusalem: Government Printer, 1932-1948.
Supplement to Survey of Palestine; Notes Compiled for the Information of the United Nations Special Committee on Palestine. Jerusalem: Government Printer, June 1947.
Supplementary Memorandum by the Government of Palestine, Including Notes on Evidence Given to the United Nations' Special Committee on Palestine up to the 12th July 1947. Jerusalem: Government Printer, 1947.
A Survey of Palestine Prepared for the Information of the Anglo-American Committee of Inquiry. 3 vols. Jerusalem: Government Printer, 1946.
Department of Statistics. *Statistical Abstract of Palestine.* 1936, 1937-38, 1939, 1940, 1941, 1942, 1943, and 1944-45. Jerusalem: Government Printer, 1937-1946.

7. *United Nations*

A/364, A/364/Add. 1, A/364/Add. 2, A/364/Add. 3, and A/364/Add. 4. *Official Records of the Second Session of the General Assembly; Supplement No. 11: United Nations Special Committee on Palestine; Report to the General Assembly.* 5 vols. Lake Success. September 3-October 9, 1947.
A/519. *Official Records of the Second Session of the General Assembly; Resolutions.* Lake Success, January 8, 1948.
A/532. *Official Records of the Second Special Session of the General Assembly; Supplement No. 1. Report of the United Nations Palestine Commission.* Lake Success, 1948.
A/544. *Official Records of the Second Special Session of the General Assembly; Report of the Trusteeship Council.* Lake Success, 1948.
A/555. *Official Records of the Second Special Session of the General Assembly; Supplement No. 2: Resolutions.* Lake Success, 1948.
A/620. *Official Records of the Third Session of the General Assembly; Supplement No. 2: Report of the Security Council to the General Assembly.* Lake Success, 1948.
A/648. *Official Records of the Third Session of the General Assembly; Supplement No. 11: Progress Report of the U.N. Mediator on Palestine.* Paris, 1948.
A/810. *Official Records of the Third Session of the General Assembly; Part I: Resolutions.* Paris, December 1948.
A/838. *Second Progress Report of the United Nations Conciliation Commission for Palestine.* Lake Success, April 19, 1949.
A/1227. *Palestine; Netherlands and Sweden: Draft Resolution; United*

Nations Protection of the Holy Places in Palestine. Lake Success, December 8, 1949.

A/1231. *Palestine; Telegram from the Minister for Foreign Affairs of the Hashemite Kingdom of Jordan Addressed to the Secretary General.* Lake Success, December 8, 1949.

A/1251. *Official Records of the Fourth Session of the General Assembly; Resolutions.* Lake Success, December 28, 1949.

A/1286. *Official Records of the Fifth Session of the General Assembly; Supplement No. 9: Question of an International Regime for the Jerusalem Area and Protection of the Holy Places; Special Report of the Trusteeship Council.* Lake Success, 1950.

A/6717. *Letter from the Minister for Foreign Affairs of the Union of Soviet Socialist Republics.* Lake Success, June 13, 1967.

A/AC.38/L.63. *Palestine; Protection of the Holy Places; Draft Resolution Presented by Sweden.* Lake Success, December 5, 1950.

A/AC.38/L.71. *Palestine; Question of an International Regime for the Jerusalem Area and Protection of the Holy Places; Draft Resolution Presented by Belgium.* Lake Success, December 12, 1950.

A/L.519. *Draft Resolution Submitted by the Union of Soviet Socialist Republics.* Lake Success, June 19, 1967.

A/L.5281/Rev. 2. *Afghanistan, Guinea, Iran, Malaysia, Mali, Pakistan, Somalia, and Turkey: Revised Draft Resolution, Measures Taken by Israel to Change the Status of the City of Jerusalem.* Lake Success, July 14, 1967.

A/PV.1525-1559. *Official Records of the Fifth Emergency Special Session of the General Assembly; Provisional Verbatim Record.* Lake Success, June 17-September 18, 1967.

S/743. *Telegram Addressed to the President of the Security Council by the Minister for Foreign Affairs of Egypt.* Lake Success, May 15, 1948.

S/863. *Text of Suggestions Presented by the U.N. Mediator on Palestine to the Two Parties on June 28, 1948.* Lake Success, July 3, 1948.

S/1264/Rev. 1. *Security Council; Official Records; Fourth Year; Special Supplement No. 3: General Armistice Agreement between Egypt and Israel.* Lake Success, December 13, 1949.

S/1296/Rev. 1. *Security Council; Official Records; Fourth Year; Special Supplement No. 4: General Armistice Agreement between Lebanon and Israel.* Lake Success, April 8, 1949.

S/1302/Rev. 1. *Security Council; Official Records; Fourth Year; Special Supplement No. 1: General Armistice Agreement between Jordan and Israel.* Lake Success, June 20, 1949.

S/1353/Rev. 1. *Security Council; Official Records; Fourth Year; Special Supplement No. 2: General Armistice Agreement between Syria and Israel.* Lake Success, 1949.

S/8146. *Security Council; Official Records; Report of the Secretary-General under General Assembly Resolution 2254 (ES-V) Relating to Jerusalem.* Lake Success, September 12, 1967.

S/8427 and S/8427/Add.1. *Letter Dated 23 February 1968 from the Permanent Representative of Jordan Addressed to the Secretary-General.* Lake Success, February 23, 1968.

S/PV.1347-1361. *Security Council; Official Records; Provisional Verbatim*

Record. Lake Success, June 5-14, 1967.

S/PV.1373-1382. *Security Council; Official Records; Provisional Verbatim Record.* Lake Success, November 9-22, 1967.

S/RES/242 (1967). *Resolution Adopted by the Security Council at Its 1382nd meeting.* Lake Success, November 22, 1967.

T/118. *Trusteeship Council; Official Records; Second Session; Second Part; Draft Statute for the City of Jerusalem.* Lake Success, January 26, 1948.

T/123. *Trusteeship Council; Official Records; Second Session; Observations of the Jewish Agency for Palestine on the Draft Statute for the City of Jerusalem.* Lake Success, February 17, 1948.

Official Records of the First Special Session of the General Assembly. 3 vols. Lake Success, 1947.

Official Records of the First Special Session of the General Assembly; Resolutions. Lake Success, 1947.

Official Records of the Second Session of the General Assembly; Ad Hoc Committee on the Palestinian Question. Lake Success, 1947.

Official Records of the Second Session of the General Assembly; Plenary Meetings. 2 vols. Lake Success, 1947.

Official Records of the Second Special Session of the General Assembly. 2 vols. and Annex. Lake Success, 1948.

Official Records of the Third Session, Part I; Ad Hoc Political Committee; Summary Records and Annexes. Paris, 1948.

Official Records of the Third Session of the General Assembly, Part I; First Committee. Paris, 1948.

Official Records of the Third Session of the General Assembly, Part I; Plenary Meetings. Summary Records and Annexes. Paris, 1948.

Official Records of the Third Session of the General Assembly, Part II; Ad Hoc Political Committee. Summary Records and Annexes. Lake Success, 1949.

Official Records of the Third Session of the General Assembly, Part II; Plenary Meetings. Summary Records and Annexes. Lake Success, 1949.

Official Records of the Fourth Session of the General Assembly; Ad Hoc Political Committee. Summary Records and Annex. Lake Success, 1949.

Official Records of the Fourth Session of the General Assembly; First Committee. Summary Records and Annex. Lake Success, 1949.

Official Records of the Fourth Session of the General Assembly; Plenary Meetings. Summary Records and Annex. Lake Success, 1949.

Official Records of the Fifth Session of the General Assembly; Plenary Meetings. Vol. I. Lake Success, 1950.

Security Council. *Official Records; Third Year.* Lake Success, 1948.

Trusteeship Council. *Official Records; Second Session; Second Part.* New York, 1948.

_____. *Official Records; Second Session; Second Part. Annex.* New York, 1948.

_____. *Official Records; Second Session; Third Part. Annex.* Lake Success, 1948.

_____. *Official Records. Second Special Session.* Lake Success, 1949.

————. *Official Records; Sixth Session.* Geneva, 1950.
————. *Official Records; Sixth Session; Annex.* Vol. I. Geneva, 1950.
Yearbook of the United Nations. 1947-1948, 1948-1949, 1950, 1952, 1953. Lake Success. Annual.

8. *United States*

Department of State. *Anglo-American Committee of Inquiry. Report to the United States Government and His Majesty's Government in the United Kingdom.* Department of State Publication 2536. Washington: Government Printing Office, 1946.
————. *Foreign Relations of the United States.* 1921, Vol. I; 1922, Vol. II; 1923, Vol. II; 1924, Vol. II; 1936, Vol. III; 1937, Vol. II; 1938, Vol. II; 1939, Vol. IV; 1940, Vol. III; 1941, Vol. III; 1942, Vol. IV; 1943, Vol. IV; 1944, Vol. V. Washington: Government Printing Office, 1936-1965.
————. *Mandate for Palestine.* Washington: Government Printing Office, 1927.
————. *Press Releases.* Washington: Department of State, 1938-1968.
————. "Telegram 82 of April 25, 1950 from the American Embassy in Amman to the Secretary of State." Plain text. Unpublished.
————. *Transcript of Press and Radio News Briefing.* Washington: Department of State, 1967-1968.
————. *United States Policy in the Near East Crisis.* Department of State Publication 8269. Washington: Government Printing Office, August 1967.

9. *Collected Documents*

Badi, Joseph, ed. *Fundamental Laws of the State of Israel.* New York: Twayne Publishers, 1961.
Bentwich, Norman, comp. *Legislation of Palestine, 1918-1925.* Vol. I. Alexandria, Egypt: Printed for the Government of Palestine by Whitehead Morris Ltd., 1926.
Doukhan, Moses, comp. *Laws of Palestine, 1926-1931.* 3 vols. Tel Aviv: L. M. Rotenberg, Law Publishers, 1933.
Huchman, Moshe, ed. *Osef Chukei Yisrael (Mihatchalat Hamandat Vead Hayom) al kol Tekuneihem.* Tel Aviv: Hachevra Lehotzaat Chukei Umishpatei Yisrael, Continuous. 8 vols.
Hurewitz, J. C., ed. *Diplomacy in the Near and Middle East: A Documentary Record.* 2 vols. Princeton, N. J.: D. Van Nostrand Company, Inc., 1956.
Majmu'at al-Qawanim wa al-Anzimah (Collection of Laws and Regulations). Vol. I. Amman: Jordanian Syndicate of Lawyers, 1957.
Whiteman, Marjorie M., ed. *Digest of International Law.* Vol. I. Department of State Publication 7403. Washington: Government Printing Office, 1963.

10. *Miscellaneous Reports*

Bertram, Sir Anton, and J. W. A. Young. *The Greek Orthodox Patriarchate; Commission's Report on Certain Controversies.* London: Oxford University Press, 1926.
Bertram, Sir Anton, and Harry Charles Luke. *Report of the Commission Appointed by the Government of Palestine to Inquire into the Affairs*

of the Orthodox Patriarchate of Jerusalem. London: Oxford University Press, 1921.

Cust, L. G. A. *The Status Quo in the Holy Places.* London: Printed by H. M. Stationery Office for the Government of Palestine, 1929.

International Commission for the Wailing Wall. *Report of the Commission appointed by His Majesty's Government in the United Kingdom of Great Britain and Northern Ireland, with the Approval of the Council of the League of Nations, to Determine the Rights and Claims of Moslems and Jews in Connection with the Western or Wailing Wall at Jerusalem.* London: H. M. Stationery Office, 1931.

B. Books and Pamphlets

Abdallah, King of Jordan. *My Memoirs Completed (al-Takmilah).* Trans. Harold W. Glidden. Washington: American Council of Learned Societies, 1954.

American Jewish Committee. *American Jewish Year Book, 1947-48.* Philadelphia: The Jewish Publication Society of America, 1947.

Antonius, George. *The Arab Awakening.* Beirut: Khayat's College Book Cooperative, 1938.

Attlee, Clement R. *As It Happened.* London: William Heinemann Ltd., 1954.

Attwater, Donald. *The Christian Churches of the East.* Rev. ed. 2 vols. Milwaukee: The Bruce Publishing Company, 1947-1948.

Avi-Yonh, Michael, David H. K. Amiran, Julius Jothan Rothschild, and H. M. Z. Meyer, *Jerusalem, The Saga of the Holy City.* Jerusalem: The Universitas Publishers, 1954.

Azcárate y Florez, Pablo de. *Mission in Palestine, 1948-1952.* Washington: The Middle East Institute, 1966.

Baedeker, Karl. *Palestine and Syria.* Leipzig: Karl Baedeker, Publisher, 1898.

_____. *Palestine and Syria.* Leipzig: Karl Baedeker, Publisher, 1912.

Barbour, Nevill. *Nisi Dominus.* London: George G. Harrap and Company, Ltd., 1946.

Begin, Menachem. *The Revolt.* London: W. H. Allen, 1951.

Ben-Gurion, David. *Israel, Years of Challenge.* New York: Holt, Rinehart and Winston, Inc., 1963.

Bernadotte, Folke. *To Jerusalem.* London: Hodder and Stoughton, 1951.

Bilby, Kenneth W. *New Star in the Near East.* New York: Doubleday and Company, Inc., 1950.

Brockelmann, Carl. *History of the Islamic Peoples.* London: Routledge and Kegan Paul Limited, 1949.

Brodetsky, Selig. *Memoirs.* London: Weidenfeld and Nicolson, 1960.

Collin, Bernardin. *Les Lieux-Saints.* Paris: Les Editions Internationales, 1948.

Crossman, Richard H. S. *A Nation Reborn.* New York: Atheneum, 1960.

_____. *Palestine Mission.* New York: Harper and Brothers, 1947.

Crum, Bartley C. *Behind the Silken Curtain*. New York: Simon and Schuster, 1947.

de Novo, John. *American Interests and Policies in the Middle East, 1900-1939*. Minneapolis: The University of Minnesota Press, 1963.

de Reynier, Jacques. *A Jérusalem un drapeau flottait sur la ligne de feu*. Neuchâtel: Editions de la Baconnière, 1950.

Elston, D. R. *No Alternative*. London: Hutchinson and Company Ltd., 1960.

ESCO Foundation for Palestine. *Palestine: A Study of Jewish, Arab, and British Policies*. 2 vols. New Haven: Yale University Press, 1947.

Evatt, Herbert V. *The Task of Nations*. New York: Duell, Sloan and Pearce, 1949.

Eytan, Walter. *The First Ten Years*. New York: Simon and Schuster, 1958.

Gabby, Rony E. *A Political Study of the Arab-Jewish Conflict*. Paris: Librairie Minard, 1959.

Garcia-Granados, Jorge. *The Birth of Israel*. New York: Alfred A. Knopf, 1948.

Glubb, John. *Britain and the Arabs*. London: Hodder and Stoughton, 1959.

Halperin, Samuel. *The Political World of American Zionism*. Detroit: Wayne State University Press, 1961.

Hanna, Paul L. *British Policy in Palestine*. Washington: The American Council on Public Affairs, 1942.

Harris, George L. *Jordan*. New Haven: HRAF Press, 1958.

Hartmann, Richard. *Palästina unter den Arabern, 632-1516*. Leipzig: J. C. Hinrichs, 1915.

Hebrew University of Jerusalem. *Israel and the United Nations*. New York: Manhattan Press, 1956.

Hitti, Philip K. *History of the Arabs*. 5th ed. London: Macmillan and Company Ltd., 1951.

Horowitz, David. *State in the Making*. New York: Alfred A. Knopf, 1953.

Howard, Harry N. *The King-Crane Commission*. Beirut: Khayats, 1963.

————. *The Partition of Turkey, 1913-1923*. Norman: University of Oklahoma Press, 1931.

Hull, Cordell. *Memoirs*. Vol. II. New York: The Macmillan Company, 1948.

Hurewitz, J. C. *Middle East Dilemmas*. New York: Harper and Brothers, 1953.

————. *The Struggle for Palestine*. New York: W. W. Norton and Company, Inc., 1950.

Joseph, Dov. *The Faithful City*. New York: Simon and Schuster, 1960.

Kirk, George. *The Middle East in the War*. Issued under the auspices of the Royal Institute of International Affairs. London: Oxford University Press, 1952.

———— *The Middle East, 1945-1950*. Issued under the auspices of the Royal Institute of International Affairs. London: Oxford University Press, 1954.

La Brière, Yves de. *L'Organisation internationale du Monde contemporain et la Papauté souveraine*. Premiere série (1885-1924). Nouvelle ed. Paris: Editions Spes, 1930.

Laqueur, Walter Z. *The Soviet Union and the Middle East.* New York: Frederick A. Praeger, 1959.

Le Strange, Guy. *Palestine under the Moslems.* London: A. P. Watt, 1890.

Levin, Harry. *I Saw the Battle of Jerusalem.* New York: Schocken Books, 1950.

Lie, Trygve. *In the Cause of Peace.* New York: The Macmillan Company, 1954.

Litvinoff, Barnet. *To the House of Their Fathers.* New York: Frederick A. Praeger, 1965.

Lloyd George, David. *The Truth about the Peace Treaties.* 2 vols. London: Victor Gollancz Ltd., 1938.

Lorch, Netanel. *The Edge of the Sword.* New York: G. P. Putnam's Sons, 1961.

Luke, Sir Harry, and Edward Keith-Roach. *The Handbook of Palestine and Transjordan.* London: Macmillan and Company Ltd., 1934.

McDonald, James. *My Mission in Israel, 1948-1951.* London: Victor Gollancz Ltd., 1951.

MacDonald, Robert W. *The League of Arab States.* Princeton, New Jersey: Princeton University Press, 1965.

Magnes, J. L., et al. *Palestine—Divided or United? The Case for a Bi-national Palestine before the United Nations.* Jerusalem: Ihud Association, 1947.

Mann, Sylvia. *Re-united Jerusalem.* Jerusalem: The Jerusalem Post, 1967.

Mantoux, Paul. *Les Délibérations du Conseil des Quatre.* 2 vols. Paris: Editions du Centre National de la Recherche Scientifique, 1955.

Manuel, Frank. *The Realities of American-Palestine Relations.* Washington: Public Affairs Press, 1949.

Marlowe, John. *The Seat of Pilate.* London: The Cresset Press Ltd., 1959.

Marriott, J. A. R. *The Eastern Question.* 4th ed. London: Oxford University Press, 1940.

Millis, Walter, ed. *The Forrestal Diaries.* New York: The Viking Press, 1951.

Monroe, Elizabeth. *The Mediterranean in Politics.* 2nd ed. London: Oxford University Press, 1939.

Moorman, John R. H. *A History of the Church in England.* New York: Morehouse-Gorham Co., 1954.

O'Ballance, Edgar. *The Arab-Israeli War, 1948.* New York: Frederick A. Praeger, 1957.

Parkes, James. *The Story of Jerusalem,* 2nd, rev. ed. London: The Cresset Press Ltd., 1950.

Pearlman, Moshe. *Ben-Gurion Looks Back.* New York: Simon and Schuster, 1965.

Pernod, Maurice. *Le Saint-Siège, l'Eglise catholique, et la Politique mondiale.* Paris: Armand Colin, 1929.

Phillips, Paul G. *The Hashemite Kingdom of Jordan: Prolegomena to a Technical Assistance Program.* Chicago: [n. pub.], 1954.

Rackauskas, Constantine. *The Internationalization of Jerusalem.* Washington: The Catholic Association for International Peace [1957].

Republican Coordinating Committee. *The Middle East—Crisis and Oppor-*

tunity. Washington: Republican National Committee, July 1967.

Robinson, Jacob. *Palestine and the United Nations*. Washington: Public Affairs Press, 1947.

Roosevelt, F. D. *The Public Papers and Addresses of Franklin D. Roosevelt*. Vol. VIII (1938). New York: The Macmillan Company, 1941.

Roth, Cecil. *A Short History of the Jewish People*. London: East and West Library, 1959.

Rouse, Ruth, and Stephen C. Neill, eds. *A History of the Ecumenical Movement, 1517-1948*. 2nd ed. Philadelphia: The Westminster Press, 1967.

Sachar, Abram Leon. *A History of the Jews*. 5th ed. New York: Alfred A. Knopf, 1964.

Sakran, Frank C. *Palestine Dilemma*. Washington: Public Affairs Press, 1948.

Samuel, Herbert Louis, Viscount. *Grooves of Change*. Indianapolis: The Bobbs-Merrill Company, 1946.

Schechtman, Joseph B. *The United States and the Jewish State Movement*. New York: Thomas Yoseloff, 1966.

Sharef, Zeev. *Three Days*. New York: Doubleday and Company, Inc., 1962.

Shwadran, Benjamin. *Jordan, A State of Tension*. New York: The Council for Middle Eastern Affairs, 1959.

Stavrou, Theofanis George. *Russian Interests in Palestine, 1882-1914*. Chicago: Argonaut, Inc., 1965.

Stein, Leonard. *The Balfour Declaration*. New York: Simon and Schuster, 1961.

Sykes, Christopher. *Crossroads to Israel*. Cleveland: The World Publishing Company, 1965.

Toynbee, Arnold. *Survey of International Affairs, 1937*. Vol. I. Issued under the auspices of the Royal Institute of International Affairs. London: Oxford University Press, 1938.

————. *Survey of International Affairs, 1938*. Vol. I. Issued under the auspices of the Royal Institute of International Affairs. London: Oxford University Press, 1941.

Truman, Harry S. *Memoirs*. 2 vols. Garden City, N. Y.: Doubleday and Company, Inc., 1955-1956.

Warren, Israel P. *Jerusalem, Ancient and Modern*. Boston: Elliot, Blakeslee and Noyes, 1873.

Watson, Charles M. *The Story of Jerusalem*. London: J. M. Dent and Sons Ltd., 1912.

Weisman, Herman L. *The Future of Palestine; An Examination of the Partition Plan*. New York: [n. pub.], 1937.

Weiss-Rosmarin, Trude. *Jerusalem*. New York: Philosophical Library, 1950.

Weizmann, Chaim. *Trial and Error*. London: Hamish Hamilton, 1949.

Welles, Sumner. *We Need Not Fail*. Boston: Houghton Mifflin Company, 1948.

Williams, Francis. *A Prime Minister Remembers.* London: Heinemann, 1961.

Williams, L. F. R. *The State of Israel.* London: Faber and Faber Ltd., 1957.

Zaar, Isaac. *Rescue and Liberation.* New York: Bloch Publishing Company, 1954.

C. Articles

Ajamian, Bishop Shahe. "Brief Notes on the Armenian People and the Armenian Patriarchate of Jerusalem," *Christian News from Israel*, XVIII, No. 3-4 (December 1967), pp. 37-40.

Cunningham, Sir Alan. "Palestine—The Last Days of the Mandate," *International Affairs*, October 1948, pp. 481-90.

FitzGerald, William. "An International Regime for Jerusalem," *Royal Central Asian Journal*, Vol. XXXVIII, Parts III and IV (July-October 1950), pp. 273-83.

Germanos, Monsignor, Archbishop of Sebastia. "The Greek Orthodox Patriarchate of Jerusalem," *Christian News from Israel*, XVIII, No. 3-4 (December 1967), pp. 22-26.

Glick, Edward B. "The Vatican, Latin America, and Jerusalem," *International Organization*, Vol. XI (1957), pp. 213-19.

Kenen, I. L., ed. "The Future of Jerusalem," *Near East Report*, January 1968, Supplement, pp. 14A-16A.

Leonard, L. Larry. "The United Nations and Palestine," *International Conciliation*, 1949, pp. 603-786.

Médebielle, Father Pierre. "The Latin Patriarchate of Jerusalem," *Christian News from Israel*, XVIII, No. 3-4 (December 1967), pp. 26-32.

Mogannam, E. Theodore. "Developments in the Legal System of Jordan," *The Middle East Journal*, V, No. 2 (Spring 1952), pp. 194-206.

Mohn, Paul. "Jerusalem and the United Nations," *International Conciliation*, October 1950, pp. 421-71.

Psomiades, Harry J. "Soviet Russia and the Orthodox Church in the Middle East," *The Middle East Journal*, XI, No. 4 (Autumn 1957), pp. 371-81.

Roosevelt, Kermit. "The Partition of Palestine: A Lesson in Pressure Politics," *Middle East Journal*, January 1948, pp. 1-16.

Samuel, Edwin. "The Government of Israel and Its Problems," *Middle East Journal*, January 1949, pp. 1-16.

Sellers, Katherine W. "Armenian Church Torn by Dispute," *The Christian Century*, LXXIV, No. 51 (December 18, 1957), pp. 1522-24.

Shultz, Lillie. "The Jerusalem Story," *The Nation*, December 17, 1949, pp. 589-91.

Shwadran, Benjamin. "Jerusalem Again," *Middle Eastern Affairs*, I, No. 12 (December 1950), pp. 357-64.

――――. "Jordan Annexes Arab Palestine," *Middle Eastern Affairs*, I, No. 4 (April 1950), pp. 99-111.

Wilson, Sir Charles W., and Sir Charles M. Watson. "Jerusalem," *Encyclopedia Britannica* (11th ed.), XV, 331-35.

Wright, Esmond. "Abdallah's Jordan, 1947-1951," *Middle East Journal*, Autumn 1951, pp. 439-60.

Yost, Charles W. "The Arab-Israeli War: How It Began," *Foreign Affairs*, January 1968, pp. 304-20.

D. Unpublished Materials

Rousan, Mohmoud Ahmad. "The Internationalization of Jerusalem." Master's thesis, The American University, 1957.

Snetsinger, John Goodall. "Truman and the Creation of Israel." Ph.D. dissertation, Stanford University, 1969.

Van Deusen, Edwin R. "The Development of Democratic Institutions in the Hashemite Kingdom of the Jordan." Master's thesis, The American University of Beirut, 1955.

E. Newspapers and Periodicals

Haaretz. August 18, 1967.

The Jerusalem Post. May 1950-February 1968.

Maariv. June 3, 1966.

New Judaea. August-September 1937.

The New York Times. June 1922-February 1968.

Oriente Moderno. October-December 1948 and April-June 1949.

The Palestine Post. January 1948-May 1950.

The Times. July 1935-March 1957.

The Washington Post. June 1967-February 1968.

INDEX

Abdallah, Amir, 26, 27
  King, 59, 62-64, 73, 74, 79-81, 90, 96, 119
Abd al-Rahim Bey, Muhammad Kamil, 79
Abramov, Alexander, 93
Abu al-Huda, Tawfiq Pasha, 64
Acre, 3, 18, 39, 43
Affula, 39
Afghanistan, 56
Allied Supreme Council, 6, 7, 19
American Christian Palestine Committee, 83, 84
American Zionist Council, 37
Amman, 26, 59, 64, 73, 83, 104, 116
Anglican Bishop in Jerusalem, 42
Anglican Church. *See* Church of England
Anglo-American Committee of Inquiry, 38, 39
Anglo-American Treaty of 1924, 20, 29, 30
Aqir, 31
al-Aqsa Mosque, 113, 116, 117
Arab Government of All Palestine, 64
Arab-Jewish Conference of 1939, 32
Arab Higher Committee, 21, 27, 40, 41, 44, 54
Arab League, 59, 63, 64, 70, 92, 114
Arab Legion, 59
Armenians, 96, 111, 112, 123
Ashdod, 43
Atarot, 104
Athenagoras, Patriarch, 106
Attlee, Clement, 37-40
Auster, Daniel, 35, 59, 80
Austin, Warren, 52, 53
Australia, 32, 41, 47, 48, 74, 76, 81, 90
Austria, 38, 120, 123
Austria-Hungary, 6
Azcárate y Florez, Pablo, 58, 59, 64

Balfour, Arthur James, 10, 13, 16
Balfour Declaration, 4, 6, 11, 19, 21, 28
Barlassina, Monsignor (Latin Patriarch of Jerusalem), 10
Beersheba, 28, 39
Beirut, 4, 70, 100
Beit Guvrin, 28
Beit Shean, 39, 40
Belgium, 47, 75, 81, 90

Benedict XV, Pope, 6, 10
Benedictos, Patriarch, 98, 99
Ben-Gurion, David, 61, 66, 67, 71, 80, 82
Ben-Zvi, Yitzhak, 93
Bernadotte, Count Folke, 57, 59-68, 119
Bertram-Luke Commission, 16
Bertram-Young Commission, 18
Bethlehem, 1, 2, 19, 23-25, 28, 39, 43, 74, 91, 110, 114-16
Bevin, Ernest, 65
Bidault, Georges, 60
Boisanger, Claude de, 70
Boissevain, G. W., 93
Borough system, 124-25
British High Commissioner in Palestine, 17, 34-36, 39, 40, 54, 64
Brotherhood of St. James, 96, 98, 112
Bunche, Ralph, 68
Burns, Sir Alan, 48

Cadogan, Sir Alexander, 41
Cairo, 58, 59, 63, 104
Cambon, Paul, 7
Canada, 41, 43, 47, 76, 79
Canterbury, Archbishop of, 74, 84
CENTO, 100
Ceretti, Monsignor, 12
Chile, 79, 93
China, 48, 57, 68
Christian interest in Jerusalem, 110-13
Church of England, 15, 74
Church of Scotland in Palestine, 42
Church of the Holy Sepulchre, 1, 14, 96, 110, 111, 123
Church of the Nativity, 1, 2, 14, 110
Church of the Virgin, 2
Churchill, Winston, 4, 10, 37
Chuvakhin, Dmitri Stepanovich, 101
Clemenceau, Georges, 5-7
Commission of the Churches on International Affairs, 83, 84
Committee for the Defense of Arab Jerusalem, 108
Condominium, 119-20
Confraternity of the Holy Sepulchre, 15, 18
Copts, 99
Corpus separatum, 48, 50, 51, 56, 61, 71, 78, 81, 86, 87, 106
Crane, Charles R., 19
Cromer, Lord (Sir Evelyn Baring), 3
Cross, Frank M., Jr., 105
Crusades, 1, 110, 114, 115, 117
Cuba, 47, 76
Customs union, 122
Custos of the Holy Land, 42
Czechoslavkia, 41, 43

Damascus, 4, 26
Damianos, Patriarch, 18
Damietta, 114
Davies, William D., 105
Dayr al-Sultan, 99
Dead Sea, 28
Defense Regulations of 1938, 35
De Gaulle, Charles, 107
Delbos, Yvon, 25
De Leon, Quiñones, 12
Denmark, 90
Derderian, Patriarch Yeghishe, 97, 98
Dewey, Thomas E., 41, 66
Displaced persons, 38, 39
Dome of the Rock, 113, 114, 116, 117
Druzes, 3
Dulles, John Foster, 93

Eban, Abba, 49, 71, 80, 82, 84-86, 88, 89, 104, 105
Eckhardt, A. Roy, 105
Eden, Anthony, 25
Egypt, 2, 4, 21, 37, 56, 58, 63, 68, 76, 100. *See also* United Arab
    Republic
Eilat, 101
Eliash, Morechai, 49, 50
El Salvador, 76
Emergency Committee, 61
Eretz Israel, 103
Eshkol, Levi, 101, 102
Ethridge, Mark, 70
Evans, Harold, 55, 56, 58, 59

Faruq, King, 63
al-Fatah, 100
Faysal, Amir, 19, 26
FitzGerald, Sir William, 36
Forrestal, James, 52
France, 1, 2, 6, 7, 14, 16, 25, 42, 47, 48, 54-57, 68, 70, 76, 78, 81,
    82, 107, 113, 120, 123
Frederick II, 1, 114

Galilee, 31, 40, 43, 59, 65, 67, 68
Garden Tomb, 123
Garreau, Roger, 82-84, 87-89
Gasparri, Cardinal, 10, 11
Gaza, 3, 64
Gaza Strip, 101, 102
General Zionists, 82
Gerig, Benjamin, 48, 49, 51

Germany, 21, 38
Germany, Federal Republic of, 107
Gharafeh, Bishop Simon, 99
Golan Heights, 102
Goldberg, Arthur, 107
Government House, 64, 65, 70, 101, 107
Grady, Henry, 39
Grant, Frederick C., 105
Great Britain, 1, 3, 5-7, 10, 11, 16, 17, 19, 25, 32, 33, 41, 43, 44, 47, 48, 52, 55, 59, 67, 69, 76, 78, 79, 81, 82, 88-91, 92, 107, 120, 123
    Palestine Partition Commission, 30-32
    Royal Air Force, 31
    Royal Commission of 1937, 21-24, 26-29, 31, 33, 113
    Secretary of State for the Colonies, 4, 10, 24, 28, 29, 52, 57
Greater Syria, 26, 63
Greece, 76, 95, 113, 120, 123
Gromyko, Andrei, 53
Guatemala, 41, 43, 45, 56, 95

Hadassah Hospital, 65
Hadera, 28
Haifa, 2, 3, 64
Haram al-Sharif, 21, 83, 96, 104, 108, 113, 114, 120-25
Harris poll, 105
Harrison, Earl G., 37
Harrison Report, 37, 38
Hashim, Ibrahim, 97, 98
Hashomer Hatzair, 27
Hebron, 28, 115
Herut Party, 82
Herzliya, 61
Hilmi, Ahmed, 64
Holy Places, 1, 3, 6-17, 19, 20, 24-26, 29, 31, 33, 42, 43, 46, 54, 62, 65, 71-73, 75, 77, 79, 83-86, 88, 89, 95, 96, 102, 104-6, 112-14, 117, 121-25
Holy Places Commission, 8-17, 111
Husayn, King of Jordan, 97, 101, 115, 116, 123
Husayn, Sharif of Mecca, 4, 26, 32
al-Husayni, Hajj Amin, 22, 27, 64

Ibn Saud, King, 63
Iceland, 45, 79
Imperiali, Marquis, 14
In Multiplicibus, 67
India, 4, 32, 41, 43, 47, 76
International Committee of the Red Cross, 64, 70
Internationalization, 43, 65, 68, 72, 74, 82-84, 107, 121, 122
    functional vs. territorial proposals, 71, 72, 73-80, 104, 107, 121
Iran, 41, 43

Iraq, 23, 26, 27, 49, 56, 58, 76
Israel, 59, 61, 65-69, 71-82, 84, 85, 88-91, 92, 95, 99-102, 104-107,
    113, 114, 116-18, 120-25
  Constituent Assembly, 92
  Knesset, 80, 82, 92, 95
  Ministry for Foreign Affairs, Liaison Office, 94, 95
  Provisional Government, 61-63, 66
Israelian, Patriarch Guregh, 96, 97
Italy, 3, 6, 16, 113, 120, 123
Izvestia, 59

Jaffa, 2, 23, 28, 40, 45
Jarallah, Husam al-Din, 64
Jenin, 28
Jericho, 28, 64
Jessup, Philip C., 57
Jewish Agency for Palestine, 22, 28, 34, 37, 41, 42, 46, 50, 53
  executive, 28, 39, 40, 44, 49, 56, 61, 118
  partition plans, 28, 40, 41
Jewish Quarter, 103, 109
Jewish interest in Jerusalem, 117-119
Johnson, Herschel, 44
Johnson, Lyndon B., 102, 104, 107, 110
Jordan, 29, 58, 62, 67, 69, 72-75, 77-82, 84, 88, 90, 91, 92, 96-98,
    100-102, 106, 113-17, 119-22, 124, 125. *See also* Transjordan
Joseph, Dov, 49, 63, 64, 66

al-Kamil, Sultan, 114
Katholikos of Echmiadzin, 97
Katholikos of Sis, 97
Kendall, Henry, 109
al-Khalidi, Husayn Fakhri, 22, 96
al-Khalidi, Mustafa Bey, 34
Khan, Inamullah, 104
Khan Yunis, 28
King, Henry C., 19
King-Crane Commission, 19, 20
Kollek, Teddy, 104
Kosygin, Alexei, 100
Kurnub, 61

Lake Tiberias, 23
Latin Christians, 1, 2, 6, 14, 19, 96, 111, 112, 120, 123
Laurentie, Henri, 48
Law and Administration Ordinance, 103
Lawson, Edward P., 93
League of Nations, 24
  Council, 9-14, 16, 17, 24-26, 33
  Permanent Mandates Commission, 17, 24-26, 33
  Secretary-General, 10, 11

171

Lebanon, 4, 26, 47, 52, 58, 67, 76, 80, 120
Lie, Trygve, 48, 53, 80
Lloyd George, David, 4-8
Lundstrom, Aage, 66

McDonald, James G., 64
McMahon, Sir Henry, 4, 26, 32
McMahon, Thomas J., 71, 72
Maghribi Quarter, 103
Malik, Charles, 76
Malta, 6
Mamilla Muslim Cemetery, 96
Mandelbaum Gate, 116
Marshall, George, 53, 65-67
Meir, Golda, 49, 61
Mexico, 48, 76, 81
Migdal, 28
Millerand, Alexandre, 7
Montefiore, Sir Moses, 118
Morrison, Herbert, 39
Morrison-Grady Plan, 39, 40
Mosul, 5
Mount Carmel, 61
Mount of Olives, 96
   Jewish Cemetery, 96, 120
Mount Scopus, 28, 31
Municipal Corporations Ordinance of 1934, 34, 35, 104
Municipal Government of Jerusalem, 23, 34, 35, 36, 54-57, 59, 62, 108
Muslim interest in Jerusalem, 113-17

Nablus, 83
al-Nabulsi, Sulayman, 97
al-Nashashibi, Raghib, 96
Nasser, Gamal Abd al-, 101
Nathanya, 61
National Council of Churches, 105
Nazareth, 18, 23, 25, 114
Negev, 31, 39, 40, 43, 46, 59, 62, 65-67
Nersoyan, Tiran, 83, 84, 97
Netherlands, 41, 43, 76, 77, 90, 93, 95, 123
Nichols, John, 93
Niebuhr, Reinhold, 105
Nitti, Francesco, 7, 8
Norway, 45, 79

Oecumenical Patriarchate, 15, 106
Orlando, Vittorio, 7
Ormsby-Gore, William, 28
Orthodox (Greek), 1, 2, 6, 15, 16, 18, 19, 67, 96, 111, 123
Ottoman Empire, 5, 9, 19, 111
Ottoman Imperial Regulations of 1875, 18
Ottoman Porte, 96

Pakistan, 115
Palestine Arab Congress, Second, 64
Pan-Arab Congress (Bludan, Syria), 27
Partition of Palestine, 23, 25-31, 40, 41-47, 69, 74, 78
Patriarch of Alexandria, 99
Patriarch of Jerusalem (Latin), 10, 15
Patriarch of Jerusalem (Orthodox), 16, 18, 120
Patriarchate (Armenian), 83, 84, 86, 96-99, 112
Patriarchate (Orthodox), 15, 83, 84, 99, 106, 112
    Arabizers vs. Hellinizers, 15, 18, 98, 99, 112, 121-23
    Holy Synod, 15, 16, 18
Paul VI, Pope, 106
Peel, Earl, 22, 31
Peel Commission, 21-24, 26-29, 31, 33, 113
Peru, 41, 43, 76
Pius XI, Pope, 10, 67
Pius XII, Pope, 67, 71
Poland, 38, 45, 55, 56
Population of Jerusalem, 34, 49, 50, 60, 61, 118, 121
Pravda, 59
Protectors, 1, 3, 122-124
Protestants, 3, 74, 110, 112, 120, 123

Qalandiya, 104
Qatamon quarter, 65

Rafah, 28, 31
Ramallah, 28, 31
Ramat Gan, 94
Ramla, 31
Redemptoris Nostri, 71
Republican Coordination Committee, 107
Revisionists, 62
Robinson, James M., 105
Roman Catholics. *See* Latin Christians
Romania, 102, 119
Roosevelt, Franklin D., 30
Ross, John C., 78, 79
Russia, 1, 2, 5, 6, 15, 34, 123. *See also* Union of Soviet Socialist
    Republics

Safad, 118
St. Jean de Maurienne Agreement, 3
St. Stephen's Gate, 102
San Remo Conference, 8
Sarona, 61
Saudi Arabia, 63
Sharett, Moshe, 49, 50, 62, 63, 66, 67, 73, 75, 88, 94, 121
Shazar, Schneor Zalman, 109
al-Shuqayri, Ahmad, 79